Wisdom for Worship

70 Reflective Assemblies

for Primary Schools

by Margaret Cooling

Stapleford Project Books

Acknowledgements

I would like to thank my husband, Trevor, for his support in the writing of this book. Thanks are also due to the following for their help with different aspects of the project: Richard Cooling, Robert Cooling, Ruth Cooper, Maggie Goodwin, Sue Hatherly, Deborah Helme, Mike Skidmore, Paul Truby and Diane Walker. I would like to express my gratitude to several Stapleford schools for allowing me to test this material and to the staff of the following schools for trialling the assemblies:

• Stevenson Junior School, Stapleford, Nottingham.

• St. Peter's Smithhills Dean Church of England Primary School, Bradford.

• Daubeney Middle School, Kempstone, Bedford.

• St. Paul's Church of England Voluntary Controlled School, Stalybridge.

• St. Clements Voluntary Aided School, Worcester.

First published 1995

ISBN 0-9516537-3-3

British Library Cataloguing in Publication Data
A catalogue record for this book is available from the British Library

Cover design and internal illustrations by Jane Taylor, Genus Art (with the exceptions listed below)

The following illustrations are by Robert Cooling:
signs, page 33
labels, page 60
mobile, page 61.

Illustration on page 61 taken from Corel Draw!

Page formatting by Mike Challen

Printed in England for
STAPLEFORD PROJECT BOOKS
Stapleford House
Wesley Place
Stapleford
Nottingham NG9 8DP
by Counterprint, Chesterfield

This book has been produced under the auspices of the Stapleford Project, a curriculum development initiative based at Stapleford House Education Centre. The Project aims to produce materials and offer in-service courses to resource the teaching of Christianity in schools. Stapleford House is the national conference and study centre of the Association of Christian Teachers. Full details of courses and publications are available from Stapleford House Education Centre, Wesley Place, Stapleford, Nottingham. NG9 8DP.

Credits

We are grateful to the following organisations for allowing us to reproduce their logos:

• Amnesty International

• The Scout Association

• The St John Ambulance

• The British Heart Foundation.

The author and publishers are grateful to the following for permission to reproduce poems:

The Bells of Heaven by Ralph Hodgson with permission of Macmillan General Books and Mrs. Hodgson

Green Blackboards by Michel Quoist with permission of Gill and Macmillan, Publishers

Extract from *A Thousand Reasons for Living* by Dom. Helder Camera with permission of Darton, Longman & Todd

Can't Be Bothered to Think of a Title by Ian McMillan with permission of the author

Extract from *Lazy Man's Song* by Arthur Waley with the permission of Harper Collins Publishers Ltd.

Contents

Words, words, words

Just thinking about it

Things to avoid

Contents

Contents

Seven things God does not tolerate

God's world

The Basic Facts: ENGLAND AND WALES

1. There must be a daily act of worship for every pupil. This can be any time of the day in any normal school grouping and should usually take place on the school premises. It is the head teacher's responsibility, or the governors in voluntary schools, to ensure this happens.

2. It must be in addition to any non-religious assemblies. Wherever possible it should be a single act.

3. The majority of acts must be wholly or mainly of a broadly Christian character meaning they should reflect the broad traditions of Christian belief. They can contain non-Christian elements, but must contain some elements which accord a special status to Jesus Christ. Worship must not be distinctive of any particular denomination.

4. Worship must be appropriate to the ages, aptitudes and family backgrounds of all pupils such that they can all take part. Decisions about the nature of broadly Christian worship will take these factors into account. Taking part implies more than a passive attendance. Collective worship should elicit a response from all pupils even though they may not all feel able to identify with a particular act of worship.

5. The aims of worship are:

'to provide the opportunity for pupils to worship God, to consider spiritual and moral issues and to explore their own beliefs; to encourage participation and response whether through active involvement in the presentation of worship or through listening to, [watching] and joining in worship offered; and to develop community spirit, promote a common ethos and shared values and reinforce positive attitudes.'

6. Worship should be concerned with reverence or veneration paid to a divine being or power. This is the natural and ordinary meaning of the word worship. It should reflect something special or separate from ordinary school activities, although it can be related to the day to day life, aspirations and concerns of the school.

7. Collective worship in schools will 'necessarily be of a different character from worship amongst a group with beliefs in common'. It is not corporate.

8. Non-broadly Christian worship is allowed:

* in a minority of acts of worship
* if a determination is granted to a school by SACRE
* if parents request and arrange it

9. Both teachers and parents have a legal right of withdrawal.

10. Worship should promote respect and understanding of those with different beliefs and religious practices.

Information compiled from the 1988 Education Act and Circulars 1/94 (England) and 10/94 (Wales)

Note: *Word in brackets only applies in Wales.*

The Basic Facts: SCOTLAND

1. In law Education Authorities are given 'liberty to continue' the custom of religious observance in schools established in the past but they cannot discontinue this customary provision without a poll of local electors.

2. In effect this means that primary schools should ensure that all pupils take part in religious observance not less than once a week.

3. Religious observance is an occasion when 'something akin' to worship takes place. It 'has a significant part to play in transcending the informative role of religious education'. Its precise form will be determined by school policy.

4. The aims of religious observance are:

'to promote pupils' spiritual development, to increase their understanding of religious practices such as prayer and meditation and the religious experience which underlies them, to promote the ethos of the school through the expression and celebration of shared values and to provide opportunity for individual reflection on spiritual and moral concerns.'

5. In non-denominational schools it should be of a broadly Christian character, reflecting the broad consensus of Christian beliefs without being specific to any one denomination. Where appropriate, special acts may be organised drawing on other religious traditions.

6. 'Active participation is essential to the quality of the experience.' The best acts develop themes carefully chosen to suit children's experience and understanding and utilise a variety of methods of presentation. There should be opportunities for the involvement of pupils.

7. School chaplains will often contribute to religious observance, remembering that it is not the same as a congregation gathered for worship.

8. Parents have the right to withdraw their children.

9. Religious observance may take place in individual classes, by stage or as a whole school.

Information compiled from HMI Report 1989, SOED Circular 6/91 and Religious and Moral Education 5-14, SOED 1992.

The Basic Facts: NORTHERN IRELAND

1. An act of collective worship must be included in every grant aided school for all pupils every day.

2. Collective worship may take place in one or more assemblies depending on the most appropriate arrangements for the school as long as every pupil attends one such assembly.

3. Parents may request that their child is wholly or partly excused from attendance at collective worship.

4. Teachers may make a request to the Board of Governors of their school to be wholly or partly excused from attending or conducting collective worship and furnish the Board with a statutory declaration that the request is made solely on the grounds of conscience.

5. Outside visitors can be invited by the Board to conduct collective worship.

6. Some suggested aims for collective worship are:

'To encourage the development of a Christian ethos throughout the school community. To help pupils see that worship of God is a relevant part of daily life. To illustrate the practical outworkings of Christianity in the lives of people. To encourage pupils to reflect on their existence, and the questions which life poses. To develop a sense of "community" in the school.'

Information compiled from The Education and Libraries (NI) Order 1986 and Transferor Representatives' Handbook (Transferor Representative Council, September 1994)

Introduction

Summaries of the legal requirements governing school worship in England, Wales and Northern Ireland and religious observance in Scottish schools, together with advice that has been issued is given on pages 1-3. These are complex, particularly in the case of England and Wales, and much ink has been spilled in trying to help schools in developing viable policies. This is not the place to pursue the intricacies of the debate, but one issue is emerging which is of such central significance that it is worthy of comment. I shall suggest that the Book of Proverbs provides a surprisingly fruitful resource for resolving a key conundrum.

SOLVING THE CONUNDRUM

The legislation applying to England and Wales and the advice issued by the Department for Education (as it was then called) in Circular 1/94 and the Welsh Office in Circular 10/94 have served to focus attention on a particular conundrum which arises out of the attempt to conduct religious worship in schools. Although this legislation and advice does not apply in Scotland and Northern Ireland, the debates that go on in these two countries show that the conundrum certainly does apply.

The heart of the puzzle lies in the fact that schools are required to fulfil two expectations at once. These are:

Firstly they are required to provide pupils with the opportunity to worship as understood in the normal and natural sense of offering reverence or veneration to a divine being or power. Furthermore the majority of the acts of worship must be of a broadly Christian character, which particularly means that they should reflect the traditions of Christian belief and must contain some elements which accord a special status to Jesus Christ. In Scotland all religious observance is meant to be of this broadly Christian character.

Secondly they are required to provide acts of worship which are appropriate for all pupils whatever their own family background. As the two Circulars put it: 'Pupils who do not come from Christian families should be able to join in the daily act of collective worship even

though this would, in the main, reflect the broad traditions of Christian belief ' (paragraph 65)

What is more the joining in that is required is more than passive attendance, but should entail eliciting a response from pupils. Hence the insistence in the Circulars that worship in schools is of a different character from that taking place within a faith community. It is therefore collective, not corporate.

The conundrum is therefore this: how can worship be provided in schools that both entails worship of the Christian God, and accords special status to Jesus Christ, whilst at the same time being such that all pupils can join in whatever their family background, be that Christian or non-Christian? The tension is between providing an act of worship which is a celebration appropriate for the whole school community and, at the same time, ensuring that worship is clearly Christian in character.

The Office for Standards in Education (OFSTED) have recognised the difficulties this creates and have suggested that schools may need to think in terms of two separate activities. In the first the emphasis will be on broadly Christian worship and in the second the emphasis will be on the spiritual and moral development of the pupils, understood in terms that apply to all human beings irrespective of religious commitment. OFSTED inspectors have therefore been encouraged to comment positively on events which promote spiritual and moral development understood in these broad and inclusive terms of reflecting human shared values, even though they may not fulfil the letter of the law requiring an act of broadly Christian worship.

THE BOOK OF PROVERBS AS A WAY FORWARD

Perhaps surprisingly, I am going to suggest that another way of resolving this conundrum is to look to using wisdom literature like the Book of Proverbs. This makes possible one act in which the twin goals of providing opportunity for broadly Christian worship and of promoting the spiritual and moral development of all pupils can be brought together. The reason for this lies in the very nature of the Book of Proverbs (see pages 7 and 8 for further details) as containing wisdom, most of which is shared by all human beings, but which is set in the context of the celebration of a relationship with God.

This book provides ideas for broadly Christian worship using individual proverbs from the Book of Proverbs to provide the themes. In developing these I have sought to highlight the shared wisdom and used this as a focus for spiritual and moral development. This has been done by using the proverb to promote self-knowledge on the part of the pupil and by employing reflective techniques which engage the emotions and feelings in responding to the proverb. At the same time I have, where appropriate, developed the fact that, as far as Christians are concerned, each proverb has its proper context in a relationship with God. So the seventy acts of worship in this book seek to bring together the aims of promoting the spiritual and moral development of pupils and of providing the opportunity for broadly Christian worship. In order to fulfil these two goals it is important to take account of a number of key issues.

KEY ISSUES

1) The importance of atmosphere

The atmosphere created is crucial to the success of an act of worship. The 'feel' will affect pupils' ability to reflect on what they see and hear. The atmosphere can be influenced by a number of factors:

a) the way pupils and staff are addressed.

b) the ethos and relationships within the school generally.

c) the room, its physical atmosphere (e.g. stuffiness), size and arrangement.

d) the use of music, drama, poetry and art as a focus for worship.

e) the presence or absence of members of staff, and their degree of involvement.

f) distracting noises.

g) the degree of comfort for staff and children.

h) the separation of the notices and discipline issues from the act of worship.

i) the way pupils enter and leave.

j) the amount of participation or passive listening.

k) the balance between talk and silence/music.

l) the degree to which there is a relaxed but ordered and secure environment.

Attention given to these factors can greatly increase the quality of an act of worship.

2) Promoting spiritual and moral development

If acts of worship are to contribute to pupils' spiritual and moral development, the religious material must relate to their own experience but must also take them beyond everyday experience so that they can reflect on their own values and beliefs in the light of the religious stimulus. Ways of creating appropriate opportunities for such reflection are suggested in this book, see pages 9-11 for further details.

Part of the task of promoting spiritual and moral development lies in developing a sense of community. Integral to achieving this is using acts of worship as a way of celebrating and affirming the values of the school community. Proverbs, with its concern for relationships in the family and the community, offers an ideal source of themes which allow community life to be celebrated and affirmed. Using pupils' work and achievements as part of the content of the act of worship further enhance this, as will involving visitors from the local community.

3) Respecting pupil integrity

Acts of worship must be appropriate to the family background of the pupils. This is integral to showing respect for the children and their parents. If a school can conduct its acts of worship in a way that models such respect, then the children too will be encouraged to be respectful to each other. There are probably three main ways of achieving this.

Firstly care should be taken to ensure that the type of participation that is required of children is appropriate in each case. It is very important to encourage participation by pupils and staff alike and joining in with music, readings and drama as well as bringing in items relevant to the theme are effective ways of achieving this. However there are clearly varying degrees of participation that are appropriate and care should be taken in ensuring the position of each child or teacher is respected. For example it would normally be quite appropriate to ask a child from a church going family to read a prayer, but insensitive to do so if the parents are atheists.

Secondly the use of non-inclusive language is extremely important. By this is meant that phrases such as 'we believe' or 'we will now pray' are avoided in preference for ones like 'Christians believe' and 'I am now going to say a prayer which is special to Christians.' Such language leaves both pupils and staff free to identify with the religious content or not as is appropriate to them.

Thirdly, but linked to our second point, is that it should be clear from the way an act of worship is conducted that pupils and teachers are free to respond in ways that are appropriate for them. Variety of response rather than uniformity should be the expectation of whoever is leading. Appropriate responses might be anything from simply appreciating that what has been said is important to Christians right through to adoration of God. By definition, worship can only be freely given, it cannot be compelled. Schools are required to provide the opportunity for worship to take place, no more. Participants are less likely to feel compromised if it is clear that a variety of responses are acceptable. In practice this will mean allowing pupils the freedom not to join in certain activities, but to listen quietly instead.

4) The Importance of Planning

There is no doubt that forward planning increases the quality of worship. There are always times when instant improvisation becomes essential, but as a policy it will

not do. Certainly OFSTED inspectors will be looking for clear and well understood policy statements which are being implemented in practice. Themes which have been decided in advance and rotas that give leaders plenty of notice are also important

It is also helpful if a system of recording is instituted. Probably the best way to do this is to have ready printed forms available which teachers can fill in quickly for recording the content of each act of worship. In time the forms can become the basis of a long term plan, with ideas that have worked well being arranged into themes. The forms can be printed five to a page to make a weekly assembly diary.

AND FINALLY

Two other important points need to be borne in mind:

1) Worship and RE are not the same

Acts of worship can certainly stimulate follow-up work for RE. They can also incorporate and celebrate work done by pupils in RE. But they are not the same as RE and must not be confused with it. The law requires both RE and worship to take place in school, but at different times. The difference is that worship is concerned with celebration of, and reflective responses to, religious themes whereas RE involves study of them.

2) Worship and Assembly are not the same

The law requires a daily act of worship, or in Scotland a weekly act of religious observance. Assemblies can take place in addition, but these do not have a religious focus and include such activities as routine notices and disciplinary matters. The difficulty is that most teachers refer to the act of worship or religious observance as assembly, both because it is less of a mouthful and because it sounds a lot more friendly. In the rest of this book we shall embrace this custom and therefore refer to what are in fact acts of worship as assemblies. However it is not to be forgotten that we are meaning the religious and not the secular version.

Why wisdom?

Introducing the Book of Proverbs

Proverbs is a book from the Hebrew Bible and the Old Testament of the Christian Bible. It is an example of a type of literature known as 'wisdom'. There are other books in the Bible which fall into this category and there are also blocks of wisdom material scattered throughout the Bible. Some of the wisdom sayings of the Bible have become an integral part of English language and British culture, for example, 'Pride comes before a fall' (page 26) and 'Love covers a multitude of sins' (page 41).

The wisdom of the Bible is personal, pragmatic and practical: it is about living in community. Sayings such as, ' Don't visit your neighbours too often, you will wear out your welcome,' (Proverbs 25.17) are common sense. Some of it probably started as traditional sayings handed down by word of mouth. Other sayings are polished and literary and may have been written for an educational purpose. The Book of Proverbs is concerned with three areas of life:

• The home - advice for parents and children

• The village - advice for living in the wider community

• The royal court - political advice

This book uses mostly the first two forms of wisdom, namely wisdom for the family and the village.

Other communities such as Egypt and Babylon, had their own wisdom literature which shared some similarities with that of the Bible. Biblical wisdom, however, starts from a different basis. It is not just about getting on in life and how to be successful. It starts from a relationship with God. Biblical wisdom deals with motive - after all, why should anyone bother to be wise? Why not enjoy being evil? The Bible's answer is God is wise: people are made in his 'image' and should imitate him. Throughout the Old Testament, people are told to imitate God: God is just, therefore people should be just. God is wise, therefore people should be wise. Biblical wisdom has a religious starting point.

Christians believe God has built a certain order into his creation. God is wise, and therefore his creation reflects that wisdom. Just as we can discover certain physical 'laws' in nature, such as gravity, so, as we experience life, we can discover certain moral 'laws' built into the structure of the universe. An example of this would be the value of honesty in relationships. In practical terms, this means that people from many different traditions often agree on certain rights and wrongs. Christians believe this is so because they reflect the way God created the world. People from different traditions have all discovered the same moral 'laws' that are built into the universe. Christians describe this as 'general revelation.' That means there are some things you can find out about God just by living in the world. The sayings in the Book of Proverbs reflect this God given human wisdom.

Underlying the Book of Proverbs is a fundamental commitment to God, although superficially it looks like common sense wisdom which can be taken at a non-religious level. It certainly contains much good advice for living which is not tied exclusively to the Jewish or Christian traditions. Many of the proverbs are universal in their application, which makes them very suitable for schools. However, on another level, the proverbs are deeply spiritual. A friendship with God is the religious framework within which to understand their full significance. Proverbs is a book on how followers of God can live alongside others with integrity and put their faith into action. It shows how a relationship with God can permeate every action and thought, hence the practical proverbs on speech, thought, weights and measures, and marriage. As such Proverbs should be understood as part of the Old Testament, which provides its wider context and which relates the history of God's dealings with Israel, particularly through the Law and the prophets.

In Western culture, wisdom is often seen as synonymous with intelligence. In the Bible, it is far more than that. Wisdom may include intelligence, but it goes beyond it to include:

a) The ability to tell the difference between right and wrong, good and evil.

b) The ability to write poetry.

c) Practical skill (technology, craft, etc).

d) Problem solving.

e) Political skill and settling legal disputes.

f) The ability to offer sound counsel and make judgements.

This book concentrates on a) and f), both of which reflect the moral and spiritual aspects of wisdom. One definition of wisdom is 'reason matured through experience.' Wisdom is also knowing how to live in right relationships with God and others. It is described as coming from God but showing itself in wise behaviour towards others. This is illustrated from the following quote from the New Testament book of James

'True wisdom which comes from God is pure, peaceful, gentle and friendly. It is compassionate, free of hypocrisy and prejudice and produces a harvest of good deeds.' (3.17)

There are three problems that can occur when using the Book of Proverbs.

a) Individual proverbs can become isolated from the rest of the Book of Proverbs and the context of the Bible as a whole. If a proverb is cut loose from its context, it can be made to mean anything.

b) Proverbs are sometimes applied, blanket-fashion, to any situation. Many proverbs were the result of specific experience. The wisdom is knowing when a proverb applies and when it doesn't! For example, the proverb 'A wise person ignores an insult' could be misused. There is a right time to ignore insults: there is also a time not to. Wisdom lies in knowing the right proverb for the situation.

c) Many of the proverbs use images and analogies which help people to understand the meaning. For example, insincerity is likened to a fine glaze on a cheap pot (page 64). However, most analogies have

a point of breakdown. For example, the shamrock can be used to explain the Trinity: the shamrock has one leaf divided into three, and the Trinity is one Godhead but three persons (Father, Son and Holy Spirit). This analogy breaks down if pressed too far: the Trinity is not small and green! (as suggested by Eric Idle in the film 'Nuns on the Run'). It is not advisable to make the analogies in this book apply too widely.

Proverbs in a Christian context.

The Book of Proverbs was originally written by and for the Jewish community. It is part of the Hebrew Bible and part of a strong Jewish wisdom tradition. As an Old Testament book, Proverbs is also part of the Christian Bible. The main difference between Jews and Christians is that Christians interpret Proverbs in the light of the New Testament. Jesus is seen by Christians as the living embodiment of God's wisdom (Mark 1.22). There are three factors which Christians believe make it possible to see Jesus in this way:

a) the content of what he taught - what he said struck people as wise.

b) the way he taught - it had a familiar form to Jewish listeners. For example, the parable is a development of the proverb.

c) the way in which he lived - he showed people how to live in relationship with God and others.

This assembly book has been specifically written to help teachers with delivering broadly Christian assemblies. Therefore the proverbs have been interpreted from a Christian perspective, in particular by linking them with Jesus and his teaching. If the proverbs were being used as part of an act of worship which was reflecting the Jewish tradition, they would need interpreting in a Jewish way and in a Jewish context, not linked to the New Testament. Both Christian and Jewish ways are legitimate ways of understanding the proverbs. However this book, in line with the requirements of the appropriate legislation, reflects a Christian understanding.

How To Use This Book

This book contains seventy acts of worship, or religious observance as they are called in Scotland, for primary schools. For ease of reference, from now I shall call them assemblies. They are based on the Bible and will contribute to a wider programme of broadly Christian assemblies which in turn might be part of a school's overall assembly plan. The assemblies are grouped according to themes. Each can therefore be used either as an individual assembly in its own right, or as part of a series on one theme. For ease of use, each assembly takes one page of the book.

1) The structure of each page

Each page has a set structure to make it easy to follow and contains the following components.

The Biblical Material

This consists of a proverb or part of a proverb. The words of the Bible have been adapted for primary school pupils. Teachers can read the Biblical proverb as it is, or, if they feel it needs simplifying still further for infants, it is easy to do so as the quotation is so short. For example, a teacher might decide to change 'Seven things God does not tolerate,' (page 69) to, 'Seven things God does not like,' for infants. The Biblical material does not usually have to be read at the beginning of the assembly. I indicate in the text where to use it, or teachers can introduce it wherever they feel it is appropriate.

You will need

Any items needed for the assembly are listed under this heading. Many of these will need collecting together beforehand. This means the assemblies are not on the whole 'instant', though some of them are, but they will be participatory. Time can be saved by keeping basic items in an assembly box. Please refer to the section 'Assembly box' on page 11. Items such as speech bubbles can be made during the assembly itself to reduce the preparation required. Pupils can help to make the visual aids needed as part of their participation in the assembly; they can also bring in many of the items to cut down on teacher preparation.

If pupils are participating in making things or bringing things in, it is essential that all health and safety guidelines are adhered to.

Introduction

This introduces the main idea contained in the proverb. This section will often include activities in which the pupils can join. It always starts with something the pupils know as a way of creating a link between human experience and the religious idea in the proverb.

Core Material

This section is usually (though not always) the place where the Biblical material is read. It makes the link between the human experience and the religious material, interpreting that material in the light of the Christian tradition.

Prayer/Reflection

This section contains a prayer or reflection. It is important that pupils have the opportunity to worship or reflect on what has been said and done. Not all will take that opportunity but it is important they have the freedom to do so.

2) Introducing Prayers to Children

If a prayer is being said, it is important that the language used to introduce it is sensitive and gives pupils the choice of taking part at a variety of levels. It could be introduced with some of the following phrases:

'I am going to pray/say/read a Christian prayer. I would like you to sit quietly with your eyes closed and listen. If you wish, you can join in with the amen at the end. Amen means "I agree."'

'I am going to read a prayer which is very important to Christians. I would like you to sit quietly with your eyes closed and listen. If you wish, you can pray silently while the prayer is read, if not just listen quietly.'

An 'Amen' has not been added to the prayers. It is left up to the teacher how they wish to end the prayer or reflection.

It is important that the child has the choice of just listening or joining in silently. In county primary schools, with children from many different faith traditions and secular backgrounds, it is not always appropriate to have children joining in prayers. Schools with a Christian tradition and Church schools have a different basis and the above does not necessarily apply.

Some prayers are active - they involve the pupils in doing more than listening. Sometimes pupils create a 'prayer board' or read prayers themselves. In these cases, it is important that pupils who take part are chosen with care and sensitivity.

Throughout the prayers, God is addressed as 'Father', 'Lord' or 'God'. This is normal Christian practice, as these are specifically Christian prayers. If teachers wish to change the way in which God is addressed, it is advisable to select a title of God normally used by Christians as these are broadly Christian acts of worship.

3) Handling reflections

Some assemblies have reflections rather than prayers though some are combined with prayers. Usually in a reflection God is not addressed directly. Reflections enable a person to think deeply and ponder what they have heard. Many of the reflections have a focus or aid which can take many forms:

• an object such as a stone or candle
• a period of silence
• a piece of music
• a poem
• a picture
• a visual aid produced during the assembly

Creating an appropriate atmosphere is very important for successful reflections. Pupils should be encouraged to sit still and focus their attention. They will not necessarily find reflection easy and will usually need assistance. In particular it will help to provide something on which they can focus their attention.

If the focus is a poem, first introduce it and explain any hard or significant words rather than interrupt the reading. Then read it several times to bring out the meaning. It will help to give your pupils a task to focus their listening. An example follows:

'Listen to the way this poet thinks about anger. This poet imagines anger as a tree. If the anger is not dealt with, it grows. Listen carefully to the way he reacts to being angry, first with his friend, and then with his enemy.'

Another possible focus is an object. Here is an example, from page 52, of how a stone and a bowl of water could be used:

'The prophet Micah said this : "Who is as forgiving as God? He delights to show mercy and hurls our wrongs to the bottom of the ocean (Micah 7.18-19)." This tells us that God forgives: it is as if he puts people's sins at the bottom of the sea and puts up a NO FISHING sign. Hold up the NO FISHING sign. If you have a bowl of water and a stone, ask the children to look at the sign and then close their eyes and listen for the splash as the stone sinks. The splash is a reminder of God's forgiveness.'

Music and art can similarly be used to provide a focus for reflection. Again it helps to provide pupils with a task. Two examples follow:

'Look at Judas' cloak in the picture and concentrate on the way it surrounds Jesus. Jesus is surrounded by deceit. Look at the cloak while the prayer is read.'

'Listen carefully to the way the composer creates a peaceful feel. Think about the peace the disciples felt after the storm. Think of a time you have felt very peaceful.'

Reflections need bringing to a close. In a prayer, the 'Amen' tells you it is over. In a reflection, be careful to tell the children how it will end. It could end with a piece of music, a recognised sound such as a shaker or a few notes on an instrument, a well-known prayer which acts as a summary, or with a form of words that will not spoil the atmosphere. For example:

'We have listened to our story, we have imagined lies as a tree and imagined the axe of truth cutting it down. As we go about our daily work, let us take with us the thought that truth is stronger than lies.'

4) Creating your own style

Every teacher has their own style and the assemblies can be adapted to suit different delivery styles and various contexts. Material can be added or omitted, depending on time available.

5) Health and safety

As in any school activity, all materials and activities should be safe. Teachers are referred to their health and safety document.

6) Assembly box

Having an assembly box makes preparation quicker. The following items should be in the box:

• Scissors.
• Thick felt-tipped pen.
• Sellotape.
• Glue stick.
• Sticky-Tack
  (reusable adhesive that
  does not mark. This comes under
  various brand names).
• Paper
  (various sizes, old pieces
  from display and scrap will do).
• A candle.
• Matches.
• A metal tray or old baking tin.
• A polythene bag containing
  sand.
• Some offcuts of card.

7) Single assemblies or themes

This book has been designed so that the assemblies in it can be used on their own or as part of a wider theme. They can be incorporated into a long term plan as part of an assembly programme.

8) Music

An index of music and a list of music books used can be found on pages 88-90. This index provides songs for each theme and indicates where a song applies to a particular assembly.

9) Photocopying

The illustrations in this book may be photocopied (single copies only) for use in the assembly. This permission extends to making one acetate for the overhead projector.

The dangerous gift

Biblical Material: Proverbs 12.18, Ephesians 4.29

'Thoughtless words can hurt as deeply as a sword but wise words can heal.'

'Use helpful words, not harmful ones: words which will build people up and do good to those who hear them.'

You will need:

- Toy weapons - sword, a bow and arrow etc.
- First aid box - include sling and bandage only.
- A small kitchen knife in a gift box: make sure this is kept safely.
- Wall-paper and a thick felt-tipped pen.

Introduction

Ask a few pupils to show some toy weapons (plastic swords etc.). Talk about the damage real weapons can do and how adults keep knives etc. out of reach for safety's sake. Show the first aid kit. Demonstrate putting on a bandage. Ask pupils about times when this would be needed. Talk about the way people use bandages etc. to help us heal when we have been hurt.

Core Material

Ask pupils what might be inside the box. Unwrap it yourself and show the knife. Ask the pupils about the uses of the knife. Explain that in order to be useful the knife has to be sharp. It would be useless if it were blunt. However, the very quality which makes the knife useful, also makes it dangerous. Teachers might want to take a little time here to remind children about not touching sharp knives.

Read the Biblical Material. Christians believe everyone was created by God and given the gift of thought and speech but people have the freedom to choose what they do with those gifts. Christians believe God made the tongue able to express the thoughts of the mind and a person's inner feelings. This ability makes speech very powerful, but without that power it would be useless. Both minds and tongues need using with care. They can wreck friendships if misused.

Just as a knife can be used to prepare food, or it can be misused and hurt people, in a similar way we can use words as weapons to hurt others or we can use them like a first aid kit - to heal people's hurt feelings.

Prayer/Reflection

Make the paper look like a wall. Explain that some people write hurtful things, but you are going to write some words that heal. Write pupil suggestions for healing words on the wall as positive graffiti. Ask pupils to select one piece of positive graffiti and close their eyes and think about times when people said something positive that helped them. Remind them after the assembly about not writing on walls.

Note. For guidance on prayers and reflections see pages 9-11.

Vinegar and soda

Biblical Material: Proverbs 25.20

'Singing songs to a person who is upset is like taking away someone's clothes on a cold day or mixing vinegar and soda.'

You will need:

- A transparent bowl or glass.
- Vinegar and bicarbonate of soda.

Introduction

Put some bicarbonate of soda into the bowl. Ask the pupils if they know what will happen if you pour vinegar on it. Pour the vinegar on and watch the reaction. Talk about the reaction with the pupils. The mixture will bubble rapidly because carbon dioxide is given off when the vinegar, which is an acid, is mixed with the bicarbonate of soda. Older pupils might like to conduct this experiment under supervision.

Core Material

Read the Biblical Material. If you are really upset, it is insensitive if someone tries to crack jokes. If people do that, they can expect a reaction. Just as vinegar and soda don't mix without causing a reaction, so a sad heart and fun don't go together. If you are light-hearted and joking with someone who is very unhappy, don't be surprised if you get a negative reaction.

In the Bible it talks about learning to 'weep with those who weep and rejoice with those who rejoice.' (Romans 12.15). That does not mean getting in the same state as they are. It means not staying detached and aloof. It is letting someone else's sorrow touch us so that we become sensitive and know the right thing to say. Sometimes we have to set aside our own joy or excitement in order to comfort others.

Prayer/Reflection

This extract of a poem by William Blake, who lived in the eighteenth century, expresses a little of that feeling. Listen with your eyes closed while it is read. Woe means trouble or sadness.
Listen for how he feels when he hears of another person's sadness.

Can I see another's woe
And not be in sorrow too?
Can I see another's grief
And not seek for kind relief?

Think about times when people have comforted you when you have been sad, or rejoiced with you when you have been happy.

Note. For guidance on prayers and reflections see pages 9-11.

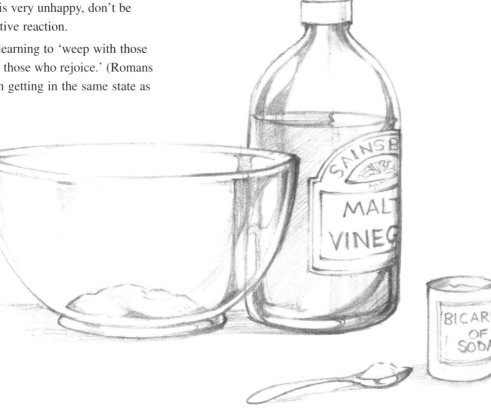

Truth

Biblical Material: Proverbs 12.19

'A lie does not last for long, but truth lasts forever.'

You will need:

• Items of different foods with 'Best Before' dates on the packaging.
• Some fragile items.
• Some tough/strong items.

Introduction

Ask some pupils to look at a number of packets and work out which has the shortest and which has the longest date life. Talk about why different foods have 'Best Before' dates. Ask pupils to sort the objects into fragile and strong. They might like to suggest situations in which the fragile items could be broken.

Core Material

Read the Biblical Material. Good and evil have different date lives. Shakespeare said, 'The evil that men do lives after them.' But the Bible says said that the good that people do lives even longer. Christians believe that good is stronger than evil, that truth is stronger than lies and all that is good and true will last forever. Compared to truth, lies are fragile, delicate and have a short date life. Christians believe truth is stronger than lies because God is truth and he lasts forever. They believe he is stronger and more powerful than anything else in this world.

Prayer/Reflection

Older pupils can create a metaphor prayer to express the strength of truth. When it is written those who wish to can join in reading the prayer. See the example below. Younger pupils can use the last two lines.

If lies are eggs, truth is an elephant.

If lies are glass, truth is steel.

If lies are weeds, truth is a lawn mower.

If lies are trees, truth is an axe.

Thank you, Father, that all that is true comes from you,

Thank you for the knowledge that truth will always be stronger than lies.

Note. For guidance on prayers and reflections see pages 9-11. Make sure all foods are within their date life.

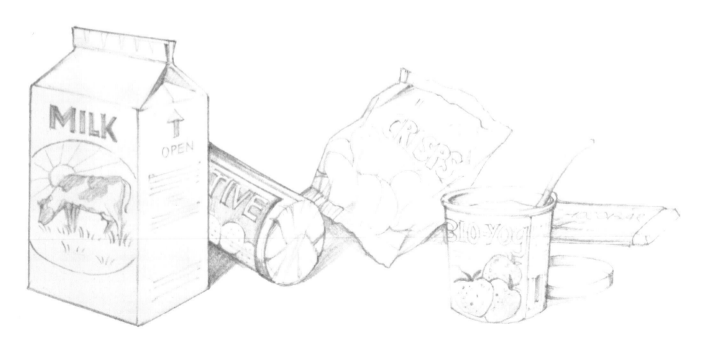

Consequences

Biblical Material: Proverbs 18.20-21

'People have to live with the consequences of what they say. Words can preserve life or destroy it, so people must accept the consequences of their words.'

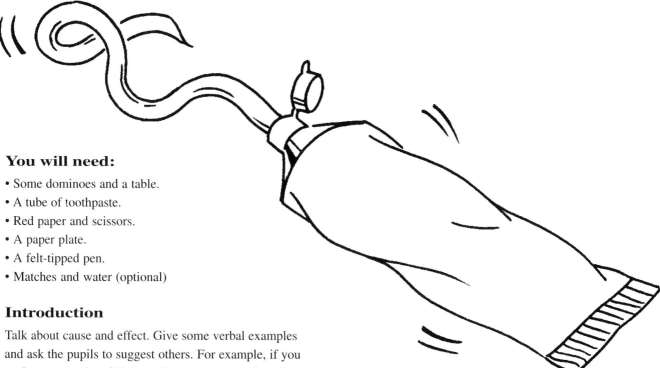

You will need:

- Some dominoes and a table.
- A tube of toothpaste.
- Red paper and scissors.
- A paper plate.
- A felt-tipped pen.
- Matches and water (optional)

Introduction

Talk about cause and effect. Give some verbal examples and ask the pupils to suggest others. For example, if you push someone they fall over. Give a demonstration of a chain of effects with the dominoes. Ask pupils to set up a line of dominoes on a table so that if they push one they all fall down eventually.

Core Material

Read the Biblical Material. Just as actions have consequences, so do words. Talk with pupils about the consequences of some words such as, 'I hate you.' Christians see words as a gift that brings responsibility. It is impossible to pretend that words don't matter - they do. Words have consequences in our own and other people's lives. The New Testament writer James likened the tongue to a flame which can start a forest fire (James 3.5). Just as carelessly throwing away a match can have terrible consequences in the form of a forest fire, so careless use of words can create damage in human relationships. Ask some pupils to cut out some red flames. Write on them some pupil suggestions of words which have bad consequences.

Once the words are out, it's hard to take them back. It can be like getting toothpaste back in a tube. Demonstrate this using the tube of toothpaste and the paper plate. If we do use words wrongly, we need to act quickly to put the situation right. It may be impossible to get toothpaste back into the tube, but it is possible to wipe up the mess afterwards.

Prayer/Reflection

Display the paper flames or ask pupils to hold them up. Ask pupils to look at the flame for a moment then close their eyes and listen to the prayer.

Like matches carelessly tossed in a forest, our words can cause great damage, destroying another person's hope and happiness. Help us, Father, to be responsible for our words.

Alternatively strike a match (preferably a long cook's match) and ask the pupils to listen to the prayer, eyes open, while the match burns.

Note. For guidance on prayers and reflections see pages 9-11.

The right word

Biblical Material: Proverbs 10.32 and 15.23

'Good people know the right thing to say.'
'It can be a great joy to find just the right word for a situation.'

You will need:

- Paper and scissors.
- Several faces (provided).
- Several coloured paper circles (draw round a cup).
- Paper and a thick felt tipped pen.
- Sticky-Tack (reusable adhesive).

Introduction

Talk with the children about going to the doctor's. When you go to the doctor, s/he does not put all the names of different medicines in a hat and pull out one by chance. S/he carefully chooses the right one for your complaint. You might like to demonstrate this. Ask the pupils to imagine that the round pieces of paper are tablets. Place them in a hat. Ask one pupil to imagine they are visiting the doctor: they can invent a minor complaint. The teacher pretends to be the doctor but instead of carefully writing out a prescription, you just pull out a paper 'tablet' at random and write a fake prescription. Ask pupils what they would think if this happened. Stress that this is NOT what the doctor does. Teachers might also like to use this opportunity to remind pupils about safety and medicines.

Core Material

Just as the doctor chooses medicine carefully, the right medicine for the right complaint, so it is important that words are chosen carefully. The right word can heal like medicine. Christians ask God for help to know the right things to say. Read the Biblical Material. Display the two faces and make two speech bubbles with pupils, placing them next to the faces What does each face express? What might be an appropriate thing to say in each case? Write suggestions in the bubbles.

Prayer/Reflection

Ask pupils to choose one of the faces to think about. Give them a few moments of silence to think about a time when they felt like the picture. What might someone have said that was appropriate to that situation?

Father, give us the wisdom to know the right words to say when people are sad and in need of comfort, or happy and want to share their joy. Forgive us for thinking that just any words will do. May we choose our words as carefully as a doctor chooses medicine.

Note. For guidance on prayers and reflections see pages 9-11.

Advice

Biblical Material: Proverbs 27.9

'Perfume smells good and can cheer you up, but good advice from a friend is even better.'

You will need:

• Some bottles of perfume / perfumed products.
• Advice columns from suitable children's magazines (optional).

Introduction

Ask pupils to come to the front and choose a product to describe, identifying its perfume by the label. For example, it might be a flower perfume such as 'Rose' or be called something like 'Sea Spray'. Talk about perfume and other perfumed products. Ask the pupils why people buy them and when people wear them. Do not remove the lids or ask the children to smell them.

Core Material

Read the Biblical Material. At first sight this looks like a very strange proverb. What have friendship and perfume got to do with each other? In Bible times, perfume often stood for joy. People wore it when they had special occasions to celebrate. We might have a shower and use some perfumed products when we are going somewhere special and have something to celebrate. The Bible is saying that it is good to have something special to cheer you up, but it is even better to have a friend who can give you good advice in times of trouble.

Some people look in magazines for advice. If you have a suitable child's magazine read a little of the letters page or show the advice column, but choose any letters/advice you read with care. People have to be careful about the advice they read: some of it may be good, but it needs checking with trustworthy people. Note: some magazines for the top of the primary age range contain advice columns.

Having a trustworthy friend who will give you good advice is valuable, but it is hard being that type of friend. Such a friendship involves being responsible. It also involves knowing when the situation, on which you are being asked to give advice, is too hard, or too serious for you to deal with and you need to go to a more experienced person.

Prayer/Reflection

Ask pupils to think quietly about times their friends have asked them for advice.

Lord, help us to be responsible friends. Give us the wisdom to know when we can give advice and when we need to ask for help. We thank you that we can ask you for help and guidance.

Note. For guidance on prayers and reflections see pages 9-11.

Gossip

Biblical Material: Proverbs 18.8

'Gossip is extremely tasty - how we like to chew it over and swallow it.'

You will need:

A selection of tasty foods such as crisps or chocolate.

Introduction

Show the various foods and talk about how tasty they are. If possible, taste some yourself and describe the different flavours. Alternatively, ask various members of staff to eat different foods and describe their flavours. Pupils can then try to guess the food from the description.

Core Material

Read the Biblical Material. The Bible describes the way some people enjoy gossip as if it were a piece of tasty food. Just as we take in food and enjoy it, so people take in gossip and enjoy it. Sometimes when a piece of gossip is heard, people go over and over it in their minds or share it with other people. It is as if it were a tasty piece of food. Some people like hearing bad news about others, about their mistakes and misfortunes: it gives them something to talk about: 'Have you heard...?' 'Did you know...?' It makes them look as if they are the people in the 'know'. It's almost as if they were talking about a new flavour in crisps instead of a person whose feelings can be hurt.

'Have you tasted the new spicy beef with pickled onion and chilli flavour crisps?'

'Have you heard what ......did?'

St. Paul, a Christian who wrote part of the Bible, talks about 'not rejoicing in wrong,' (1Corinthians 13.6). That means not enjoying other people's misfortune. Every time a person hears unpleasant gossip about someone else, they need to think about how they would feel if they were the person being discussed. Jesus laid down a 'golden rule' (Matthew 7.12). He said this. 'Do to others what you would want them to do to you.'

Prayer/Reflection

Teachers can fill in the gaps using names which do not occur in their school. This prayer can be read by the teacher or pupils can read alternate lines.

Have you tasted the new spicy beef crisps?
Have you heard what .....did?
Have you seen the latest film?
Have you heard about ......?
Have you listened to the latest CD?
You'll never guess what ....said!
Have you played the new computer game?
I bet you don't know about...?
Father, forgive us if we discuss other people like items of food or entertainment.

Note. For guidance on prayers and reflections see pages 9-11.

Speak up

Biblical Material: Proverbs 31.8

'Speak up for those who cannot speak up for themselves.'

You will need:

• The logo of Amnesty International. (provided)
• Other logos and symbols. (two provided).
• An Amnesty candle (optional) or a plain white candle.
• A tray of damp sand.
• Matches

Introduction

Show the various logos/symbols (except the Amnesty logo) and ask the pupils to guess what organisations they represent or what the symbol means.
The logos can be enlarged.

Core Material

Show the Amnesty International logo. Ask the pupils what it might mean. What do they think the barbed wire stands for? What do they think the candle represents?

On June 25th 1867, barbed wire was invented. It was used to stop cattle roaming too far on American ranches. Today it forms part of the Amnesty International logo. The wire represents the camps, prisons and cells in which many prisoners are kept. Some of these prisoners have not done anything wrong: they merely differ from the government of their country. Some have dared to speak out against injustice. Some are religious prisoners, imprisoned for their faith.

The candle was originally chosen by the founder of Amnesty International (Peter Benenson) on the basis of a proverb: 'It is better to light a candle than to curse the darkness.' Amnesty International tries to protect those who cannot speak up for themselves. Amnesty makes the plight of many of these prisoners known and works to get them released.

Read the Biblical Material. In the Bible, God is often described as the God of the stranger, the fatherless and the widow. It is a way of saying that he is particularly

concerned to defend those who have no one to speak up for them. We, too, can speak up for others when we see people treated badly. It takes courage to speak for others and wisdom to know how to do it safely and effectively. Teachers may like to talk about telling members of staff when pupils see someone treated badly.

Prayer/Reflection

If you have an 'Amnesty candle' place it in the tray of damp sand and light it. Ask the pupils to think quietly about people who need others to speak up for them. If you do not have an Amnesty candle, light an ordinary candle.

'We thank you God, that you particularly care for those who cannot speak up for themselves. Give us the courage to speak on their behalf when their voice is silenced.'

Note. For guidance on prayers and reflections see pages 9-11. Remember to extinguish the candle.

Addresses:
Amnesty International, British section, 99-119 Rosebery Avenue, London EC1R 4RE.

Candles can be purchased from them or from Articles of Faith, Bury Business Centre, Kay Street, Lancashire Bl9 6BU.

Quarrels

Biblical Material: Proverbs 17.14

'The start of a quarrel is like the first crack in a dam; stop it before it develops into a fight.'

You will need:

- Paper and scissors.
- Sticky-Tack (reusable adhesive).
- A bicycle (optional).
- A thick felt-tipped pen.

Introduction

Demonstrate riding the bike and putting on the brakes, or ask a pupil to do so if there is space to do this safely. Ask pupils how the brakes work and why we need them. Talk about the way quarrels start. Pupils can make a few speech bubbles and suggest some of the things people say which start quarrels.

 I told you so

 That's stupid

Core Material

Read the Biblical Material. Fights are not inevitable. They can be stopped: people can 'put the brakes on.' Not all arguments are bad. Sometimes it is right to have a disagreement, it stops the other person treating you or others badly. This proverb is not talking about those occasions but when quarrels move into violence.

Human beings don't come equipped with brakes in quite the same way as a bike. Ask the pupils for suggestions concerning what we could use as 'brakes' in a quarrel. They should remember that a brake is just something that stops the movement. What can people do to stop a quarrel moving into a fight?

- You can walk away. Remove yourself from the situation.
- Change the subject and think/talk about something else.
- Distract yourself. Do something to take your mind off it.
- Ask God for help.

It is hard to put the brakes on speech and action. Christians find this as hard as anyone else. It takes a life-time to learn.

Prayer/Reflection

Ask pupils to think about times when quarrels have grown into fights while a short piece of 'angry music' is played such as 'Mars' from 'The Planet Suite' by Holst. Fade out the music and read the prayer.

Like a crack in a dam growing until the dam collapses, so our quarrels often grow into fights. Give us the courage to act, God. Teach us not to be helpless victims of our anger.

Note. For guidance on prayers and reflections see pages 9-11.

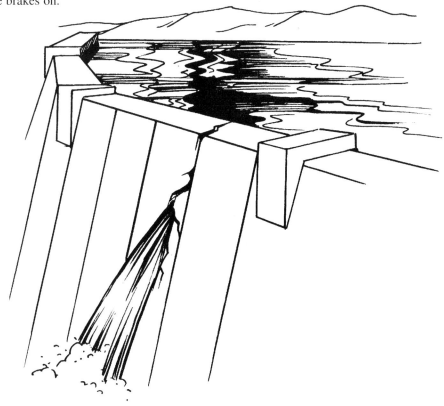

Be careful how you think

Biblical Material: Proverbs 4.23

'Be careful how you think: your life is shaped by your thoughts.'

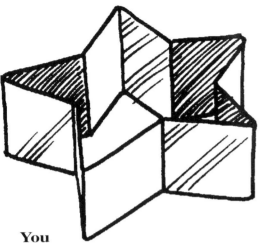

Jesus said it was not enough to avoid being violent towards others. He taught people to avoid the thoughts that lead to violence. Jesus said it was not enough to avoid treating others badly: he taught people to avoid the thoughts which lead to the bad treatment of others.

You will need:

• Plasticine or play dough.
• Some objects to press into it: cutters, pencils etc.

Introduction

Take the plasticine/play dough, and ask some pupils to create different shapes using the various items. Show the finished items and describe the way different tools and objects shaped the plasticine into the finished product. We can tell from the shape in the plasticine which object was pressed into it. Show the pupils a number of pieces of plasticine and ask them to guess from the shape which item was used to cut it or to impress a pattern on it.

Core Material

Read the Biblical Material. Just as plasticine is shaped by being pressed and moulded by other things, so our lives are shaped or moulded by our thoughts. If people think life is just about having a good time, they will live one way. If people think life is about serving God and others, it will change how they live. Thoughts matter. Thoughts may be invisible but they are extremely powerful. Lasers are also invisible, but some can cut and shape steel.

Prayer/Reflection

Ask pupils to think about the things that influence how they think: television, other people, advertising, films and music. As an optional extra teachers might like to show short extracts of videos, adverts and television programmes and play some music. Make sure all extracts are suitable and the equipment is available for the assembly. The following prayer can be said.

Like unseen hands, our thoughts shape our lives.
Behind each destructive life,
Lie thoughts even more destructive.
Behind each loving life,
Lie thoughts that create an oasis of care.
Help us to take care of what we think, Father.
It is not enough to take care of our actions.

Note. For guidance on prayers and reflections see pages 9-11.

What others think

Biblical Material: Proverbs 29.25

'It is unwise to worry about what others think of you: it's safer to trust God.'

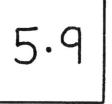   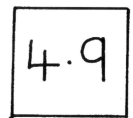

You will need:

Some pieces of card cut to represent the score cards which were once used by judges in ice skating competitions.

Introduction

Talk about ice skating and how the judges award marks. Skaters are marked out of six rather than ten. Six is a perfect score. The skaters are judged by experts and the scoring depends on their judgement. Note: with younger children leave out the decimal points.

Core Material

In life, there is no panel of experts who can hold up cards to tell people how they are doing: whether their behaviour is good or bad. Describe a few situations to the pupils and ask them to award marks from 1-6. An example would be, 'A person comes into school late because they overslept, but tells the teacher the bus was late.' Explain that 1 is a low mark and 6 is high.

It is right to take notice of trustworthy people when thinking about how to behave, but Christians believe other people's judgements are not enough on their own - they might be wrong. Read the Biblical Material. If you only rely on other people to guide you in life, you could end up constantly changing your actions to suit others as this story demonstrates.

Once an old man and a young man set out to go to market with their donkey. The young man rode the donkey, the old man walked beside it. 'What a selfish young man,' said one person, so the young man got off and let the old man ride. 'What an inconsiderate old man,' said the next person. So they both got on the donkey. 'What cruel people overloading that poor donkey,' was the next comment. The two men looked at each other and got off the donkey. 'What stupid people: fancy having a donkey and both walking!' commented a passer-by.

Worrying about other people's opinions, can lead to people being swayed first one way, then the next. Christians believe that what really matters is what God thinks. People should do what is right even if other people do not agree.

Prayer/Reflection

Pupils can hold up the score cards as the prayer is read.

1 out of 6. *There are times when we all deserve a score of 1. Forgive us when we fail, Lord.*

3 out of 6. *Sometimes we achieve a 3. We try hard, Lord, but know we can improve with your help.*

6 out of 6. *Nobody is perfect, Lord, but we know you rejoice in our progress.*

Note. For guidance on prayers and reflections see pages 9-11.

Think before you answer

Biblical Material: Proverbs 15.28; 18.13

'People with a good heart think before they answer.'
'Listen before you answer. To speak before listening is stupid and insulting.'

You will need:

- A battery.
- Wire.
- A bulb.
- Some paper clips.
  to make a simple
  circuit.

Introduction

Show how the circuit
works and how the
bulb will fail to light
if the circuit is
broken at any point.
Break the circuit in a
number of ways and
ask the pupils to look to
see if they can tell where it
is broken.

Core Material

Human bodies have something like a circuit. Just as the bulb needs to be connected to the battery, so in a similar way the mouth needs to be connected to the brain.

Unfortunately some people's mouths still work even if not connected to the brain, unlike the light. Some people speak without stopping and thinking about what they are saying. Read the Biblical Material. Whenever people speak about anything of importance, they should check they have connected their brains first and thought about what they are going to say. Christians also try to connect to God before they answer. This does not mean they pray every time they open their mouths! Christians believe that one of the ways God speaks to people is through the Bible. Christians read the Bible regularly so that they get to know God. This knowledge helps them when they speak.

Prayer/Reflection

This is a well known Christian prayer written in the sixteenth century. Pupils can listen quietly or it can be sung softly. The tune can be found in many traditional hymn books.

God be in my head,
And in my understanding;
God be in mine eyes,
And in my looking;
God be in my mouth
And in my speaking;
God be in my heart,
And in my thinking;
God be at my end
And at my departing.

Note. For guidance on prayers and reflections see pages 9-11.

Think before you act

Biblical Material: Proverbs 13.16

'Wise people are careful to stay out of trouble, but stupid people are careless and act too quickly.'

You will need:

A glove with some stickers on for eyes, mouth etc.

Introduction

Introduce your puppet - give him/her a name. Hold the glove limply, do not put your hand inside. Try to get the glove to wave to the children. It must refuse to do anything you ask it. Ask your puppet to run, jump, dance, hit you etc. All the time the glove must hang limp.
Finally ask it what the matter is: it can whisper to you or the pupils can tell you what is wrong.

'My glove puppet says it has no mind of its own, it needs someone else's hand to control it.'

Either put the glove on yourself or ask one of the children to put it on. Now tell the glove to do things. Demonstrate it running, jumping etc.

Core Material

Our hands and bodies do not act by themselves, they are guided by our minds, just as the glove puppet is guided by the hand and the mind of the puppeteer. Some people do not use their minds before they act. They act first and think afterwards. It's like a hand running free with no mind to guide it. Actions, like words, need careful thought, and if our minds control our actions, it is very important that we watch what we put into our minds. Read the Biblical Material. The Bible says this: 'Fill your minds with things that are good and deserve praise, things that are true, noble, right, pure, lovely and honourable.' (Philippians 4.8).

Prayer/Reflection

Ask pupils to look at their own hands for a moment, in silence. Hold up the glove puppet and read the prayer. Ask pupils to listen to the prayer with their eyes open, using the glove puppet as a focus.

Our hands do not have a life of their own,
They are ours to guide
Our bodies do not have a life of their own,
They are ours to guide.
Thank you Father, for minds and hearts to guide our bodies.

Note. For guidance on prayers and reflections see pages 9-11.

Pride

Biblical Material: Proverbs 16.18

'Pride and arrogance lead to a downfall.' (Pride comes before a fall)

You will need:

• Two balloons.
• A large transparent plastic bag.
• A pin.

Introduction

Blow up the balloon and talk about it being full of air: that is what makes it grow larger. Balloons are, however, fragile. Ask pupils what might happen to them. If you leave them, they slowly go down. You can also burst them with a pin. Warn the children before you do this. Place the balloon inside a plastic bag and pop it inside the plastic bag so that the pieces do not fly everywhere. If very young children are present or someone is frightened by this, omit popping the balloon.

Core Material.

Read the Biblical Material. Some people are full of their own importance as a balloon is full of air. They think they are wonderful, better than anyone else. You may wish to draw a face on another balloon at this point, or show the proud face on page 71. Such people are in danger. If people walk around with their nose in the air, looking down on others, they won't see the holes in the road! Teachers may like to arrange for some pupils to demonstrate this. Pupils can pretend to walk into things: they can look down on people and then pretend to have trodden in a puddle or mud. If people go through life boasting how good they are, they won't make friends and will look stupid when they make a mistake.

There is a right type of pride, and a wrong variety. It is right to be proud of work you have done: it is wrong to boast about it and use it to put other people down. Pupils may wish to think about things they have done of which they are rightfully proud. They could also suggest the type of things a very proud person might say which would hurt others.

Prayer/Reflection

Ask the pupils to look at the inflated balloon. The balloon is in danger of popping: people who are proud are in danger of having no friends. Older pupils can listen to the extract of a poem by John Bunyan, a seventeenth century Christian.

He that is down needs fear no fall,
He that is low no pride;
He that is humble ever shall
Have God to be his guide.

Father give us the right type of pride in our work and ourselves. May we never use pride to hurt others.

Note. For guidance on prayers and reflections see pages 9-11.

Gloating

Biblical Material: Proverbs 24.17

'Don't be glad when your enemy meets disaster, and don't rejoice when he stumbles. God knows when people gloat and does not like it.'

You will need:

• A large copy of the gloat (provided).
• Paper and a thick felt-tipped pen.

Introduction

When someone we do not like gets into trouble, it is tempting to gloat - to think they deserve it and to enjoy their misery. 'Serves them right,' we think. 'I told you so.'

Core Material

Read the Gloat poem and ask the pupils what they think the gloat might look like. They might like to draw their impression of a gloat. Show the picture, (enlarged or put on an acetate). This is how one person imagined a gloat. Ask the pupils what type of person a 'Gloat' might be.

The Gloat

The Gloat is an appalling creature
Be careful that it does not eat yer!
Its eyes are round, its lips are thin
And carved into a pompous grin.
Its head is large - it swells with pride
And nose in the air through life it glides.
Its frequent cry I'm sure you know:
It is, of course, 'I told you so.'

Read the Biblical Material. Jesus told a story about gloating.

'Once a religious leader and a tax collector went into the Temple to pray. The religious leader looked up to heaven and said, " I thank you God that I am not like other people. I don't steal or cheat like everyone else. I'm not like that tax collector over there." The tax collector stood at a distance and was so ashamed that he could not even look up. "Forgive me, God," he said. "I've done so much wrong." It was the tax collector who was right with God, said Jesus.' (Luke 18.9-14).

The religious leader had avoided many bad things. He did not steal etc, but his attitudes were wrong: he gloated over the wrong of another person. In the Bible, it makes it clear that good actions are not enough, attitudes matter as well.

Prayer/Reflection

Using ideas from the assembly, pupils can create an acrostic prayer or use this one.

Gentle, make us gentle towards others.
Love, love must be the rule.
Attitude, attitudes matter.
Obedient, obedient to the golden rule:
'Treat others as you would want to be treated.'

Note. For guidance on prayers and reflections see pages 9-11.

Laziness: learn from the ants

Biblical Material: Proverbs 6. 6-11

'Lazy people should learn from the ants. They have no ruler but they store up their food in the summer ready for the winter. How long will lazy people stay in bed? Are they ever going to get up? "Just a bit longer in bed," they say. Yet while they sleep, poverty attacks like a thief.'

You will need:

- A picture of an ant. (enlarged).
- Circles of paper and a thick felt-tipped pen.
- Ribbon or wool.

Introduction

Talk about ants and the way they organise themselves and show the picture. If there was a competition for hard work, ants would win it. If there were Olympic medals for laziness, what 'sports' would there be? Ask the pupils for suggestions. For example, you could have a gold medal for laying in bed. Create some medals with the pupils and display them. If there was a competition for laziness, this person would win it.

Can't be Bothered to Think of a Title
by Ian McMillan

When they make slouching in the chair
an Olympic sport
I'll be there.

When they give out a cup
for refusing to get up
I'll win it every year.

When they hand out the gold
for sitting by the fire
I'll leave others in the cold.

And when I'm asked to sign my name
in the Apathetic Hall of Fame
I won't go.

Core Material

Read the Biblical Material. Ants live together in communities and depend on each other as we do. One person's work - or lack of it - affects others. In the Bible, laziness is a person's failure to use their gifts, including the gift of time, for God, others and even

themselves. Laziness is not to be confused with rest. The Bible has a very positive attitude towards rest.

Prayer/Reflection

Write the word ANT in large coloured letters, then add the rest of the lines. Pupils can be encouraged to reflect on these three things about ants.

h**A**rdworking
thi**N**k ahead
work **T**ogether

Note. For guidance on prayers and reflections see pages 9-11.

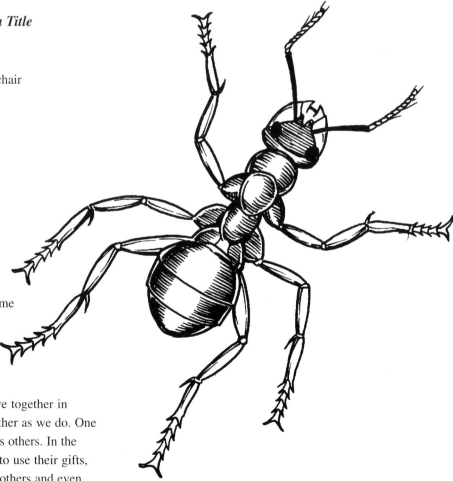

Laziness: laziness is irritating

Biblical Material: Proverbs 10.26

'Waiting for a lazy person to do something for you will be as irritating as smoke in your eyes or vinegar on your teeth.'

You will need:

• A 'No Smoking' notice (provided).
• Objects to illustrate the poem (optional).

Introduction

Ask several pupils to do some quick and easy jobs such as picking up litter at the back of the hall, or delivering a message: prime them beforehand NOT to do as you ask. Talk about how irritating it is if you ask someone to do something and they are too lazy to do it. The Bible says it is like getting smoke in your eyes. Read the Biblical Material. Talk briefly about being in smoky rooms: show the 'No Smoking' notice. Some pupils might be able to share their experiences on smoky rooms.

Core Material

Some people forget to do what you ask, others fail deliberately: they are just too lazy to do it, like the person in this poem. This poem can be read by eight pupils, holding up appropriate objects (optional).

Lazy Man's Song

1) I could have got a job, but am too lazy to choose it; *(Newspaper)*
2) I have got land, but am too lazy to farm it. *(Trowel)*
3) My house leaks; I am too lazy to mend it. *(Hammer)*
4) My clothes are torn; I am too lazy to darn them. *(Sock)*
5) I have got wine, but am too lazy to drink; *(Glass)*
5) So it's just the same as if my cup were empty.
6) I have got a lute, but am too lazy to play; *(Guitar)*
6) So it's just the same as if it had no strings.
7) My family tells me there is no more steamed rice; *(Rice or a bowl)*
7) I want to cook, but am too lazy to grind.
8) My friends and relatives write me long letters; *(Letters)*
8) I should like to read them, but they're such a bother to open.

Po Chü-I (772-846) Trans. Arthur Waley (extract).

Laziness is one way of saying, 'I don't care,' for work can be one of the ways people show they care. If, when asked to do something, a person gets on and does it, it is a way of saying, 'You matter.' People show by their actions what they think of others. The Bible says 'Love should not be just words and talk, to be real it must show itself in actions.' (1 John 3.18).

NO SMOKING!

Prayer/Reflection

Read the poem again and ask the pupils to listen silently. While they are listening ask the children to think about the man's laziness and those people who were affected by it.

Father forgive us for thinking we are totally independant and that our actions do not affect others.

Note. For guidance on prayers and reflections see pages 9-11 .

Deception

Biblical Material: Proverbs 6.12-14

'Stupid people go around telling lies. They wink with their eyes and beckon with their fingers. They make gestures to deceive people, all the while planning evil and stirring up trouble.'

You will need:

Pictures of hand signals used by police to guide traffic. The ones supplied can be enlarged.

Introduction

Show hand signals and demonstrate them or ask pupils to demonstrate them. With younger pupils, some children could pretend to be cars while others act as traffic control. Explain what each gesture means. Gestures are a form of silent language. They can be positive, like the hand signals the police use for guiding traffic in order to prevent accidents, or they can be negative. Negative gestures are ones that lie or insult people.

STOP -
traffic approaching from behind

STOP -
traffic approaching from front

BECKONING ON -
traffic approaching from side

BECKONING ON -
traffic approaching from front

Core Material

Read the Biblical Material. There is more than one way of lying. Gestures can lie. A person can lie by the actions they do, not necessarily by anything they say. A person can wink and laugh, making out something is a joke when it is really very serious. People can fool others into thinking that stealing is all right by making gestures, such as chicken noises, that indicate you are a coward if you don't join in. There are many types of lies. People can lie without ever opening their mouths. Ask pupils to suggest ways people can use gestures to lie. You might like to demonstrate some of these. For example - people can open their eyes wide and look innocent when they are really guilty. People can point to a person and indicate that they started a fight which they didn't.

Prayer/Reflection

Ask pupils to think about lies that are told by gestures. Gestures can also be used for good, like the police signals. Ask pupils to make a 'stop' signal with their hand, as shown in the illustration, then close their eyes and think about a time when they were glad that someone stopped them doing something that would have got them into trouble.

Note. For guidance on prayers and reflections see pages 9-11.

Blowing your own trumpet

Biblical Material: Proverbs 27.2

'Let other people tell you how good you are, ... never do it yourself.'

You will need:

• Well done stickers (provided).
• Some praise comments from pupil books.

Introduction

Everybody likes praise, it makes us feel appreciated and encourages us. Ask the pupils to read some of the good comments they get in their books.

'Brilliant work'
'Really good'
'You have worked hard.'

Show the stickers people can get for good work. The ones drawn can be enlarged. Would it mean much to make up praise and write it yourself? Ask the pupils what they would write in their books if they could. Why does it mean more if someone else writes encouraging comments?

Core Material

Read the Biblical Material. Some people spend time praising themselves. They tell everyone how great they are. It is right to be proud of good work or good behaviour, but it is not right to boast. Christians believe that God notices when people use their God-given gifts, whether that be in work, or in daily life. They believe praise should come from him and from other people.

This means people need to take notice of each other, and encourage each other with praise. One follower of Jesus was nick-named 'Barnabas' which means 'the encourager' because he encouraged and praised people.

Prayer/Reflection

Declare a 'Barnabas' day, when everyone makes a special effort to encourage others. Give pupils a few minutes silence to think about how they will do this.

The following prayer can be said.

Someone else thought I did well today. I thought so too, but I was not sure. I need their 'well done!' I need encouragement to keep trying. Most of all I need your 'well done!' God: it is not enough to rely on my own judgement. I might think too much, or too little of myself.

Note. For guidance on prayers and reflections see pages 9-11.

Jealousy

Biblical Material: Proverbs 27.4; 1Corinthians 13. 4; James 3. 14, 16

'Anger is cruel and rage is destructive, but they are nothing compared to jealousy.'

'Love is not jealous....'

'Don't let boasting rise from jealousy and selfishness... for where there is jealousy and selfishness there are all kinds of wrong.'

FLAMMABLE

IRRITANT

You will need:

Danger signs (provided).

Introduction

Ask pupils what danger signs are for. How many of them could draw a danger or warning sign? It could be a sign warning people that something is harmful to swallow or flammable. The two signs provided can be used. Explain that there are some things in life that are dangerous but they do not all have a danger or warning sign on them. Jealousy is dangerous. When someone is jealous they are resentful, bitter and envious of someone else. They may be jealous of someone else's looks, toys, abilities or friends. Explain that today's story is about jealousy: it is the story of Joseph and his brothers (Genesis 37).

Core Material

Joseph had ten older brothers but Joseph was very spoilt. His father, Jacob, gave Joseph a special coat and treated Joseph differently to his brothers. Joseph did not help by telling his brothers about his strange dreams, in which he dreamt that everyone would bow down to him. Joseph obviously felt he was the most important person in the family. Joseph's behaviour caused his brothers to become jealous. They became so jealous, they plotted to kill him. Reuben, the eldest brother, tried to save Joseph - as did his brother Judah. Reuben had him put in a pit

and planned to rescue him later, but while he was away, Joseph was sold as a slave to some wandering merchants.

This is an extreme example of jealousy. Most people don't try selling their little brothers or sisters! Jealousy is sometimes felt, even when there is no good cause, but the Biblical advice is to treat it as a dangerous substance. Show the danger signs again and see if the pupils can remember what they warn about. Jealousy is dangerous because it wrecks friendships and makes people bitter. We can't always help feeling jealous but we can help how we behave.

Prayer/Reflection

Ask pupils to hold up the danger signs as a focus.The other pupils can look at the signs then think quietly about the dangers of jealousy.

Not every danger in life comes with a warning sign, help us to recognise jealousy and deal with it rather than act upon it.

Note. For guidance on prayers and reflections see pages 9-11.

Anger

Biblical Material: Proverbs 30.33

'Churning milk produces butter. Hitting someone on the nose makes it bleed. Stirring up anger causes trouble.'

You will need:

- A packet of butter .
- A large lidded jar.
- Some 'gold top' milk. } optional

Introduction

Show the butter and talk about how it is made. If you have the milk, demonstrate this by pouring the top of the milk into the jar and shaking it. Pupils can take turns at shaking the jar. Explain that eventually it would turn into butter, but it would take a lot of shaking.

Core Material

Most actions have results. The result of churning the milk is butter. The result of being hit on the nose is a nose bleed. The result of stirring up anger is trouble. Read the Biblical Material. The Bible does not condemn all anger: there is the right sort of anger - anger against wrong - and a destructive type of anger. The Bible's advice on destructive anger is to deal with it quickly and calm the situation down. In the Bible it says, 'Don't let the sun go down on your anger.' (Ephesians 4.26) In other words deal with it before night, don't brood on it.

There is also a right type of anger. Jesus was very angry when he went to the Temple and found the courtyards had been turned into a market. This was the only public place some people had to pray. Some stall holders were not only selling animals and changing ordinary money into Temple money, they were cheating people as well. Jesus overturned the tables in his anger and said, 'It says in the Bible that God's house should be a house of prayer, you have turned it into a den of thieves!' (Luke 19.45,46).

Prayer/Reflection

Ask the children to sit and think about times when they have been angry and it has been the right type of anger: anger against wrong. Remind them there is also a wrong or destructive type of anger. A poet called William Blake imagined destructive anger (he calls it 'wrath') as a tree. Listen carefully to this extract from one of his poems called 'Poison tree', and note how he deals with anger towards his friend and his enemy. He uses the word 'foe' to describe his enemy. Omit the poem with younger children.

I was angry with my friend:
I told my wrath, my wrath did end.
I was angry with my foe:
I told it not, my wrath did grow.

Help us, Father, to cut down the tree of destructive anger and never to encourage it to grow.

Note. For guidance on prayers and reflections see pages 9-11

Two things I require

Biblical Material: Proverbs 30. 7-9

'Two things I ask of you, O Lord: keep lies from me: give me neither poverty nor riches-
give me only my daily bread, otherwise I may have too much and forget you.'

You will need:

• A fairy wand (a silver star/ tinsel on a wooden spoon).
• A felt-tipped pen and large sheet of paper.

Introduction

Show your magic wand and ask the pupils what they would wish for if they were given two wishes. Write up their suggestions.

I would wish for
• New trainers
• A bike
• To go on holiday

Explain that you cannot grant their wishes as your wand does not work. Pupils can come and test its lack of power by trying to turn teachers into frogs etc.

Core Material

Read the Biblical Material. Ask the pupils what two things the writer asked of God. Why do you think he asked for those two things? This person wanted to be honest and avoid lies, and he also wanted enough wealth to be safe from poverty, but not too much. Long before the Proverbs were written, the Israelites had been warned that wealth can be dangerous. It can spoil relationships with other people and God if it is not handled wisely. People who win large amounts of

money sometimes find it is very unsettling. You might want to refer to the lottery here and the Church's call for smaller amounts of prize money to be shared by a larger number of people. Friendships can be spoilt by sudden wealth. It takes a truly wise person to handle large amounts of money.

Prayer/Reflection

Ask the pupils to close their eyes and think about the things they wish for when day dreaming.

Father we often day dream about wealth, we thank you for what we have, and when we have more than we need give us the generosity to share it.

Note. For guidance on prayers and reflections see pages 9-11.

Meat or veg?

Biblical material: Proverbs 15.17. Proverbs 17.1

'Better to eat vegetables with your friends and those you love than to eat finest meat where there is hatred.'
'Better a crust of dry bread in a peaceful house than fine foods in a quarrelsome one.'

You will need:

- Several sheets of paper.
- A thick felt-tipped pen.
- Some popular foods.

Introduction

Talk with the pupils about their favourite foods and show some of the foods you have brought in. Ascertain the pupils' favourite foods using a show of hands, and create a list. Teachers may wish to talk about healthy eating at this point.

Favourite Foods

Chocolate
Strawberries
Chips
Chicken

Core Material

Ask the pupils to imagine that they have two invitations to parties. One will have all their favourite foods but the people they usually quarrel with will be there. The other has simpler food, but all their friends will be there. Two invitations can be made with the pupils during the assembly. Inside a sample menu can be written. Ask the pupils to think quietly about which party they would want to attend. Ask for arguments for and

against going to each party. Read the Biblical Material. The Bible puts people before food, money or possessions. If people used the Bible to decide which party to attend, then which party would they go to? Why does it put people before food?

Prayer/Reflection

Ask pupils to think about their favourite foods then listen to the prayer.

People first:
When other things tempt us, let us never forget
People first.
Toys or food, money or clothes
May we never put 'things' in the place of people,
Make us people people, God.

Note. For guidance on prayers and reflections see pages 9-11.

Riches

Biblical Material: Proverbs 28.6; Matthew 6. 19-21

'Better to be poor and honest than rich and dishonest.'

'Don't spend all your time storing up riches on earth. Such riches can be eaten by moths, destroyed by rust or stolen by robbers. Store up riches in heaven instead, where there are no moths, rust or robbers. Where your riches are, there will your heart be.'

You will need:

- Some clothes - fashionable.
- Some money.
- Toy car.

Introduction

If you have time you can arrange a 'clothes show.' This can be done with the pupils as commentators on clothes which can be held up by other pupils. Teacher's can bring in some items of clothes. Explain that some people put all their efforts into making money, then spend it on expensive clothes and expensive cars. The Bible is not against wealth. Wealth used rightly can make a tremendous difference to people's lives. That is why the Bible emphasises giving. The Bible has two principles concerning wealth:

1) it must be gained honestly.
2) it must be shared.

they would be poor in the Bible's terms. Money without self respect and real friends is just another form of poverty. You may like to read Matthew 6.19-21 here. This puts the emphasis on building riches of friendship and integrity.

Some people, once they have gained wealth, spend all their time and energy keeping it. Talk with the pupils about storing money, clothes and cars and what happens to them (go out of date, rust, get stolen).

Core Material

Read the Biblical Material. Riches in the Bible are always seen as coming in two forms: there are riches made up of money and objects (clothes, cars etc.) Show some of the things you have brought in. There are also invisible riches made up of things such as friendships, personal qualities (honesty etc), and a relationship with God. If a person has the first type but not the second,

Prayer/Reflection

Listen to a suitable extract of a song about money such as 'Money Money Money' by ABBA.

When people try to tell us that money is all that counts, help us, Father, to count our wealth in friends, goodness and friendship with you. Give us the wisdom to value honesty and love as a great treasure.

Note. For guidance on prayers and reflections see pages 9-11.

You can't take it with you

Biblical Material: Proverbs 11.4

'Wealth will do you no good when you die!'

You will need:

- A suitcase.
- Paper, and a thick felt-tipped pen.
- Sweets made by Cadbury and Rowntree.
- Sellotape and scissors. (optional)

Introduction

When we arrive in the world, we arrive with nothing. Babies do not arrive with a suitcase full of things they might need. If babies could choose what they could bring into the world, what do you think they might bring? Open the suitcase and write the pupil's suggestions on pieces of paper and ask them to come up and place them in the suitcase or tape them inside the open lid. If no one suggests money, add it yourself.

Core Material

Read the Biblical Material. The Bible does not condemn money or possessions, it reminds people that they came into the world with nothing and they leave it with nothing. The Bible says that people need to concentrate on what they do with their money and possessions during their lives. Jesus told a story about this called 'The rich fool.' (Luke 12. 13-21).

'Once there was a rich farmer. He had many fields and workers. One year, the harvest was particularly good: he had so much grain his barns were full and overflowing. He did not share the extra grain. Instead he said, "I will pull down my barns and build bigger ones. I will take life easy and enjoy myself. "You fool!" said God. "What will happen when you die? Who will enjoy all this wealth you have kept

for yourself?" That night the man died: he never did enjoy his wealth.

'He was a rich man in other people's eyes,' said Jesus, 'but poor in God's sight.'

Money is important: it can change people's lives. Show the sweets. The Rowntree and Cadbury families were both Christians. Both families made money in their business, but they did not keep it all for themselves, they used their money to help others. They built good homes for their workers, and decent factories. They built clinics and schools. They took to heart the saying, 'You can't take it with you,' and tried to do good with their money in their life time. Money that they did not spend was left in trusts to do good after their death. The money made by the Rowntree and Cadbury families is still helping people today.

Prayer/ Reflection

Use the suitcase to focus attention. Ask the pupils to think of the money and goods we accumulate in life.

Father, when we have the choice between being givers or hoarders, teach us to give as generously as you give to us.

Note. For guidance on prayers and reflections see pages 9-11.

Giving to God

Biblical Material: Proverbs 19.17; 14.31.

'When you give to people in need, it is like lending to the Lord.'

You will need:

- A drink of water.
- A shirt.
- A piece of bread.

Introduction

Show the different items and ask the pupils to suggest situations when they would be needed.

Core Material

The Bible suggests that every time someone who is ill, poor or in need is helped, it is as if God himself were treated in that way. The Bible also stresses putting right the situation which caused the poverty in the first place. Read the Biblical Material. Jesus told this parable to help people understand.

The parable of the sheep and the goats (Matthew 25.31-46).

'One day, God will separate people just as the shepherd separates the sheep and goats. The good people he will put on his right hand and say, "Come and be with me forever, for when I was hungry you fed me; when I was thirsty, you gave me a drink; when I was a stranger you took me in; when I was naked you clothed me; when I was in prison, you visited me."

The good people will say, "When did we see you hungry or thirsty, sick or in prison?"

God will reply, "Whenever you did this for the least of my brothers, you did it for me."

To those on his left hand, God will say, "Go away from me. When I was hungry you gave me nothing to eat. When I was thirsty you gave me no drink. When I was naked you did not clothe me; when I was a stranger you did not welcome me. When I was sick and in prison you did not visit me."

Those on God's left hand will say, "But when did we ever see you hungry or thirsty, naked or sick, a stranger or in prison?"

God will reply, "Every time you did none of these things for the least of my brothers, you failed to do it for me."'

Mother Teresa looks after the poor, sick and hungry people of Calcutta. She treats every person as if they were Christ. In that way, every person is treated with dignity and respect.

Prayer /Reflection

Read slowly the line from the parable, 'Whatever you do to the least of these my brothers you do to me.'

Lord give us the eyes to see you amid the rags.
To care for you in the sick.
To welcome you in the stranger.

Note. For guidance on prayers and reflections see pages 9-11.

Looking after your heart.

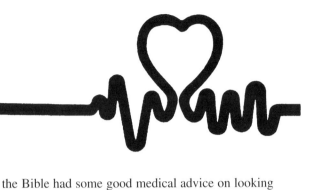

Biblical Material Proverbs 14.30, 17.22.

'A peaceful heart gives the whole body life.'

'A cheerful heart is good medicine.'

You will need:

• A skipping rope.

• Some healthy foods. Choose from the following:

Fruit.

Low fat yoghurt.

Baked beans (reduced salt and sugar variety).

Vegetables.

Whole-wheat breakfast cereal.

Introduction

Talk about looking after your body by healthy eating and exercise. Some pupils might like to demonstrate skipping. Show some of the foods and ask who likes various foods. Pupils can suggest different types of exercise they could take: swimming, football, dance, netball etc. Ask pupils which sports they enjoy.

Core Material

Long before doctors knew about ways to keep healthy,

the Bible had some good medical advice on looking after the body. Exercise is good for you (particularly your heart) and so is the right diet. The Bible reminds people that how we feel emotionally also matters.

Doctors now know that how we feel affects our health. Positive feelings such as happiness, peace and freedom from worry help our bodies in the battle to stay healthy. It has been shown that laughter and cheerfulness improve some people's symptoms of illness, especially pain. Laughter really is good medicine. Note for teachers: This should not be interpreted to mean that every time we feel unhappy we are in danger of being ill. It is merely saying that long-term stress etc does not help.

Christians believe God created people with bodies, and looking after our bodies is important. It is through our bodies that we express love and care towards others. Part of our care for our bodies should be healthy eating and exercise but we should also take care of how we feel. We can reduce some of the negative feelings such as hatred and jealousy, and cultivate positive experiences such as laughter, peace and love. For example, when we do something silly and have a choice between laughing at ourselves and getting in a temper, we can choose to laugh.

Prayer/Reflection

Ask pupils to think quietly about situations where they have had a choice in the responses they have made.

Thank you, Father for the gift of our bodies. Help us to look after them and treat them with respect, for it is with our bodies that we show others we care.

Note. For guidance on prayers and reflections see pages 9-11.

Love

Biblical Material: Proverbs 10.12

'Love covers many wrongs.'

You will need:

- A tablecloth.
- A sheet of paper.
- A table, blackboard, flip chart or similar object.
- A thick felt-tipped pen or chalk.

Introduction

When we don't like someone, we notice all the things they do wrong. We note all their faults and start to list them in our mind. Pupils can suggest faults or use the ones below, then place the list on the table or write the list on the board/chart.

1. Monday - she didn't play with me.
2. Tuesday - deliberately ignored me at lunch time.
3. Wednesday - she laughed at my painting.
4. Thursday - boasted about her new clothes.

Core Material

Once people get into this state of mind, the list keeps growing. It is difficult to break the pattern. One loving act of kindness can, however, break the pattern and make us feel differently about a person.

Read the Biblical Material. Ask a pupil to place the tablecloth over the table/chart and cover the list. Love is like this: it covers all the wrongs. In the Bible, the word 'cover' is used to describe part of the process of forgiveness. The Bible links seeing and behaving. If people constantly see other people's faults in their 'mind's eye', and dwell on them, it is likely to affect how they behave towards them. Love 'covering' the faults means faults are not constantly seen and dwelt upon, which can help prevent people acting towards others in an unloving way. Please make it clear to children that this does not mean tolerating wrong.

Prayer/Reflection

Hold up the tablecloth while the prayer is said, then cover the list again.

Love is like a tablecloth:
It covers many things.
What our eyes do not see,
Our mind does not dwell on.
And hate does not grow into actions.
Help us, Father, to use love to cover wrong.

Note. For guidance on prayers and reflections see pages 9-11.

Work

Biblical Material: Proverbs 16.3

'Ask God to bless your work, depend on him in what you do.'

You will need:

• Some job adverts..
• Objects to reflect various types of work - waged or unwaged : school work, work at home etc.

Introduction

Ask pupils to show the objects and ask with what jobs they are associated. Discuss with pupils the various types of work, and the people for whom we do jobs. Does the person for whom we do a job affect how we do it? If the Queen asked you to do a job, would it be better done than if a friend asked?

Core Material

Read the Biblical Material. Christians believe that work can be done for God, even the humblest task. They talk to God about their work and ask him to bless it. Christians do not separate their work life from their friendship with God, this makes any task special. Pupils might like to read or sing the poem below during assembly, if appropriate. It should be sung with plenty of percussion to accompany it. Instruments can be given out during the assembly.

Oh, you gotta get a glory
In the work you do;
A Hallelujah chorus
In the heart of you.

Paint, or tell a story,
Sing, or shovel coal,
But you gotta get a glory,
Or the job lacks soul.

Anonymous

Prayer/Reflection

A Christian poet called George Herbert wrote a poem to express the idea that all work should be done as if it were being done for God. Christians often sing it as a hymn. Pupils can listen while it is read or they might like to sing it as a prayer.

Teach me, my God and King,
In all things thee to see,
And what I do in anything,
To do it as for thee.

Note. For guidance on prayers and reflections see pages 9-11.

Music by Sue Hatherly

Oh, you got-ta get a glo-ry ———— in the work you do ————

A Hal-le-lu-jah cho-rus ———— in the heart of you ————

Paint, or tell a sto-ry ———— Sing or sho-vel coal ————

But you got-a get a glo-ry ———— or the job lacks soul ————

Caring for animals

Biblical Material: Proverbs 12.10

'A good person takes care of their animals.'

You will need:

• The school pet or a goldfish. (Make sure all animals are safe and children are not allergic to them)
• Paper and a thick felt-tipped pen.

Introduction

Ask the pupils about their pets. List some of the different types. Ask the pupils what you have to do to look after a pet. What are its needs?

Core Material

Read the Biblical Material. Christians believe that animals were created by God: they should be looked after for their own sake and also because God took the trouble to make them. They believe that if God thought they were worth making, they are worth caring for. Christians believe people were given a special responsibility for looking after the world of animals by God. Christina Rossetti, a Christian poet, said this about caring for animals:

Hurt no living thing:
Ladybird nor butterfly,
Nor moth with dusty wing,
Nor cricket chirping cheerily,
Nor grasshopper, so light of leap,
Nor dancing gnat, nor beetle fat,
Nor harmless worms that creep.

Prayer/Reflection

In the following poem the writer, Ralph Hodgson, imagines that God would ring the bells of Heaven with joy if people came to their senses and looked after animals. Explain any difficult words. The poet is angry that the animals are ill-treated. Children can listen silently for the names of ill-treated animals.

The Bells of Heaven

'Twould ring the bells of Heaven
The wildest peal for years,
If Parson lost his senses
And people came to theirs,
And he and they together
Knelt down with angry prayers
For tamed and shabby tigers,
And dancing dogs and bears,
And wretched, blind pit ponies,
And little hunted hares.

Father hear our angry prayers. We feel sad
and angry for animals which are ill-treated.
We pray for the work of the PDSA and
the RSPCA who care for the animals
you created.

For guidance on prayers and reflections
see pages 9-11.

Good actions

Biblical Material: Proverbs 20.11. Matthew 7. 16-20

'People show what they are by what they do.'

'You will know what people are like by the fruit they bear.'

You will need:

- A magnifying glass (optional).
- An orange or apple.
- Large felt-tipped pen (optional).
- Paper and scissors (optional).
- A plastic drinking glass with fingerprints on it.

Introduction

Ask pupils to name some television detectives. Ask them about the sort of clues detectives look for when a robbery has been committed. Give pupils the glass and the magnifying glass and ask them to find the fingerprints.

Core Material

Finding out what a person is like on the inside (their true character) is rather like being a detective. A magnifying glass is no use in this situation. It can't see into people's minds and hearts. How do you tell what someone is like on the inside? What clues can we look for? Ask the pupils for suggestions.

We usually have to work out someone's character from their actions. Read the Biblical Material. If someone produces loving behaviour, they are probably not an evil person. Jesus said a person is like a tree. You tell what type of tree it is by its fruit - an orange tree produces oranges, apple trees, apples. Good trees produce good fruit, rotten trees produce rotten fruit. In a similar way you tell a person by their actions. Good people produce good actions. In the Bible, it lists some of the good actions or 'fruits' that should grow on the 'tree' of a person's life. Pupils can cut out some simple apple shapes and write on them the Biblical 'fruits'. The 'fruits' mentioned in the Bible are: love, joy, peace, patience, kindness, goodness, faithfulness, humility and self control (Galatians 5. 22-23).

Prayer/Reflection

Nine pupils can each hold a paper apple with one of the Biblical 'fruits' on it. Each pupil can say the one line which goes with the fruit. After the prayers, ask the

pupils to select one 'fruit' and think about ways in which they could help it grow in their lives.

As we grow in your garden, Lord. Help us to produce good fruit - the fruits of:

Love, our world is desperate for love.

Kindness, the daily acts of practical love which make the world a better place.

Patience, enjoying the time you give us, not anxious to be on to the next thing.

Self control, gaining control over our own behaviour.

Faithfulness, being loyal to those we love.

Peace, bringing peace to those around us.

Joy, rejoicing in the good things in life.

Goodness, practising goodness in daily life.

Humility, holding a right view of ourselves: created, special but not perfect.

Note. For guidance on prayers and reflections see pages 9-11.

Do good when you can

Biblical Material: Proverbs 3.27-28

'Whenever you can, do good to those in need. Never ask someone to wait until tomorrow if you can help him or her today.'

You will need:

- A calendar.
- Paper and a large felt-tipped pen.

Introduction

Hold up the calendar and ask the pupils to guess what special day it is. Do this assembly when it is NOT a special day. After they have failed to guess, tell them it's St. Tib's day. Ask how many have heard of St. Tib. Tell them that St. Tib is an imaginary all purpose saint. Tib can be old or young, short or tall. Her day (she is possibly female as 'Tib' was a pet form of Isabel), can be any day of the year. Pupils might like to make an identikit picture of this all purpose saint. Traditionally, St. Tib's day is not before but not after Christmas and not Christmas day. St Tib's day is never. She is the patron saint of 'maydos' - people who 'may do' some good one day if they get round to it: people who always put off doing good or forget.

Core Material

Read the Biblical Material. Talk about the way people often fail to do good, not because they don't want to but because they don't get round to practically organising it. Good intentions and sympathy are not enough. People can't eat good intentions. The Bible's advice is never to leave to tomorrow any good that can be done today. John Wesley, a Christian who lived in the eighteenth century, had this as his rule:

Do all the good you can,
By all the means you can,
In all the ways you can,
In all the places you can,
At all the times you can,
To all the people you can,
As long as ever you can.

It is a good rule to have for each day, though if everybody did what good they could every day, St. Tib would be a redundant saint. Maybe her day would become February 30th.

Prayer/Reflection

Ask pupils to think about the opportunities for doing good which might occur today.

May do, might do, will do - some day.
Should do, ought to, will do -some day.
Meant to, would have, should have - too late.
Father help us never to postpone to tomorrow any good we might do today.

Note. For guidance on prayers and reflections see pages 9-11.

True beauty

Biblical Material: Proverbs 31.30; 1 Peter 3.3-4

'Charm can be deceptive, good looks don't last.'

'Your beauty should be an inner beauty, your true self, the beauty of a gentle and quiet spirit, which is ageless. Such beauty is of great worth in God's sight.'

You will need:

• Some make up.
• Best clothes.
• Mirror and a comb.
• Magazine images of beauty (optional).
• A large picture of a Yemeni bride (provided).

Introduction

Talk with the pupils about the lengths to which people go to make themselves handsome / beautiful. Demonstrate (on yourself) with make up if appropriate. Brush your hair and put on your best clothes or come wearing your best clothes. Show the magazine pictures. However hard we try, most of us don't look like the magazine images, because people who look like that are rare. Constantly seeing such images encourages people to spend a lot of time and money on their looks. Teachers may want to add extra material about the pressures of advertising at this point. Pupils can bring in magazine images and adverts.

Core Material

In Biblical times, people cared about their looks too. Show the picture of the Yemeni bride. We do not know exactly how people dressed in Bible times, but it may have been a little like this for very special occasions such as a wedding. The Bible puts emphasis on inner beauty. Read the Biblical Material.

In God's eyes, what matters is what we are like on the inside. There is a story in the Bible which illustrates this, in 1Samuel 16. 1-13. When the prophet Samuel went to choose a new king, God told him to choose David. David was young and inexperienced. Samuel was puzzled. 'Why choose David?' he asked. 'You look on the outside,' said God. 'I look on the heart.' David had an inner strength and an inner beauty that God could see.

A beautiful character after a while begins to show on the outside. Most faces improve with a smile . Even the most beautiful face is ruined by a sneer. We are not responsible for the looks with which we were born. We do bear some responsibility for the type of person we are inside. Christians ask God's help to change to be a better person on the inside.

Prayer/Reflection

Ask the pupils to look at the magazine pictures, if you have them, then close their eyes and listen while you read the prayer.

We can't all be handsome or beautiful. Give us an inner beauty, Lord: eyes that show compassion, mouths that smile in welcome, lips that speak the truth.

Note. For guidance on prayers and reflections see pages 9-11.

Honesty

Biblical Material: Proverbs 16.11

'God wants weights and measures to be honest and accurate and every sale to be just'

You will need:

Some scales and some items to weigh.

Introduction

Ask pupils to help you weigh the items. Cheat by pressing on the scales when you weigh them or using weights that are incorrectly labelled. Explain afterwards that you deliberately cheated and ask pupils to weigh the items again, saying by how much they were robbed by you. Explain that it is against the law to alter weights. Scales have to be regularly tested.

Core Material

Read the Biblical Material. Normally people are told not to copy, but in the Bible it teaches people to copy or imitate God. Christians believe they should be totally honest in all they do because God is honest. They should be fair because God is fair. This doesn't only apply to the big things in life, but to every action. When this proverb was written, having honest measures and fair sales was very important indeed. Most people had very little money. If they used what little money they had to buy food for the family, they would go hungry if they were cheated out of some of the food. The prophet Amos had this to say about the injustice and dishonesty going on in his day:

'You don't know how to be honest!
You don't treat the poor fairly and you rob them of their food.
You walk all over the needy.
You overcharge, use false weights and alter the scales to cheat your customers.'
(Amos 5. 11-12, 8. 5-6)

Amos knew that God cared as much about justice and fairness in everyday life as he did about the big events. God cared about shopping as well as prayer.

Prayer/Reflection

Ask pupils to close their eyes and think of the ordinary things they will do today: work, play, eat, sleep etc.

Father, we thank you that you care about all parts of life, the ordinary and the special. You care about the food we need and the way we are treated in shops. You even care that weights and measures are fair in case we are cheated. Thank you that you care about people shopping as well as people praying.

Note. For guidance on prayers and reflections see pages 9-11.

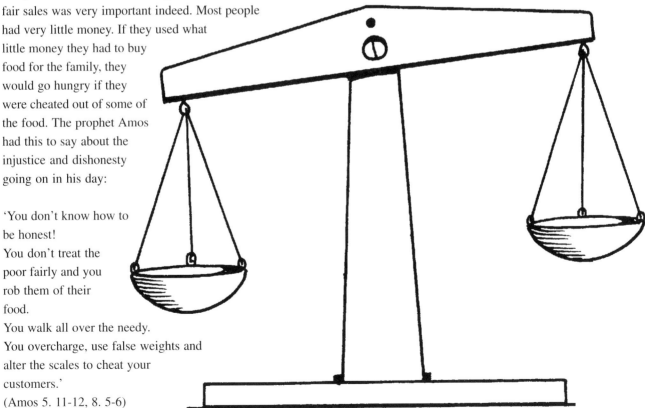

Being dependable

Biblical Material: Proverbs 25.19

'Depending on an unreliable person in a difficult situation is like trying to chew with a wobbly tooth.'

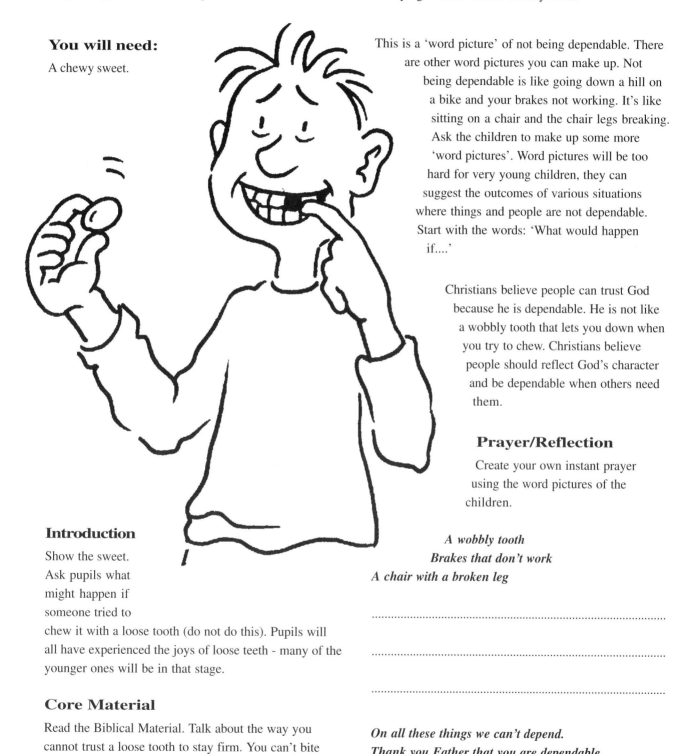

You will need:

A chewy sweet.

This is a 'word picture' of not being dependable. There are other word pictures you can make up. Not being dependable is like going down a hill on a bike and your brakes not working. It's like sitting on a chair and the chair legs breaking. Ask the children to make up some more 'word pictures'. Word pictures will be too hard for very young children, they can suggest the outcomes of various situations where things and people are not dependable. Start with the words: 'What would happen if....'

Christians believe people can trust God because he is dependable. He is not like a wobbly tooth that lets you down when you try to chew. Christians believe people should reflect God's character and be dependable when others need them.

Prayer/Reflection

Create your own instant prayer using the word pictures of the children.

Introduction

Show the sweet. Ask pupils what might happen if someone tried to chew it with a loose tooth (do not do this). Pupils will all have experienced the joys of loose teeth - many of the younger ones will be in that stage.

A wobbly tooth
Brakes that don't work
A chair with a broken leg

....

....

....

Core Material

Read the Biblical Material. Talk about the way you cannot trust a loose tooth to stay firm. You can't bite hard or chewy things with it. Pupils will probably be only too happy to share their experience of wobbly teeth.

If you try to rely on a person and they let you down, it's like a loose tooth letting you down when you try to eat.

On all these things we can't depend.
Thank you Father that you are dependable.
May we never to be a wobbly tooth to others.

Note. For guidance on prayers and reflections see pages 9-11.

Long lasting good

Biblical Material: Proverbs 10.7

'Good people will be remembered. They will be seen as a blessing, but evil people will soon be forgotten.'

You will need:

- A jar of marmalade.
- An orange.
- A can of food (optional)
- A packet of dried food (optional)

Introduction

Show the pupils the orange and ask pupils how they could make it last without it going bad. Show the marmalade and talk about the way the orange is preserved by boiling it in sugar. Ask the pupils what would happen to the orange if it was just left. Explain that other types of fruit are preserved as jam. Some pupils may have seen members of the family making preserves and be able to share that experience. Talk about other ways of preserving food, freezing, drying etc. Ask pupils for some suggestions and show some of your examples if you have them.

Core Material

Goodness, unlike fruit, cannot be preserved in sugar. You can't put it in a can, freeze it or dry it. But the Bible says that goodness does last. Read the Biblical Material. Goodness is preserved in the lives of people who experience and remember the goodness of others. Goodness changes people. It makes their lives better and makes them better people. They in turn may treat others better because they feel secure and loved, and so the chain goes on. Christians believe goodness lasts because God is the source of all goodness and he lasts forever.

Some people have epitaphs written about them. Explain what an epitaph is and read the example given concerning Thomas Hood. The best type of epitaph is written not in stone, but in the lives of other people.

Prayer/Reflection

Ask the pupils to close their eyes and silently say thank you for any good people they have known and would like to remember. We build memories of ourselves in other people by the way we live now. Some pupils might like to think silently about the way they would like to be remembered by others.

Thank you Father that no act of kindness or goodness is ever wasted, but is preserved in the lives of others.

Note. For guidance on prayers and reflections see pages 9-11. This assembly touches on the subject of death and needs sensitive handling,

'Here lies the Reverend Thomas Hood who while he lived was always good.'

Be a light

Biblical Material: Proverbs 13.9; Matthew 5.14-16.

'People are like a lamp shining brightly.'

'You are like a light for the world..... No one lights a lamp and hides it under a bowl. Lamps are placed where they can give light to the whole room. In the same way you must shine like a light before others.'

You will need:

• A torch.
• A candle in a tray of damp sand.
• A bucket (metal or plastic).
• Matches.

Introduction.

Ask pupils, in turn, to come to the front and turn on the torch, saying when they would use it. Several pupils can do this citing different situations. Talk about finding your way in the dark with a torch. Ask when they may need a candle. Share experiences of power cuts.

Core Material

Read the Biblical Material. The Bible talks about goodness as a light. Shakespeare used a similar saying, in the play, 'The Merchant of Venice'. One of his characters comments on a candle and says, 'So shines a good deed in a naughty world.'

Sometimes people do not know what to do or which way to take in life. When someone shows others how to behave by setting a good example, they are acting like a light or a torch. A torch shows us the way to go at night: a good person can show us the way to live.

Jesus told people to shine out clearly, their behaviour setting a shining example to others. You may wish to introduce some examples of people who have been 'shining examples' to others. Jesus warned people against hiding their 'light' under a bowl.

Demonstrate this by taking a large bucket and placing it over a torch or place a metal bucket over a candle. Under a bucket, a torch is no use to anyone. Similarly, if a person does not show others how to live by their good example, it's like putting a torch under a bucket: it's no use to anyone there.

Christians have often used the image of a light in their songs of worship, from the Victorian song 'Jesus bids us shine', to songs such as 'This little light of mine.' (Both are in Junior Praise, details in Music Index.). Pupils might like to sing one of these if appropriate.

Prayer/Reflection

Light the candle. While the children are looking at the candle, ask them to think of people who have set a good example to them, for whom they can say thank you.

For those who have set us shining examples of how to live, we thank you. Give us the strength, God, to be responsible and set an example to others.

Note. For guidance on prayers and reflections see pages 9-11. Remember to extinguish the candle.

Forgiveness

Biblical Material: Proverbs 17.9

'If you forgive someone when they do wrong, you make a friend.'

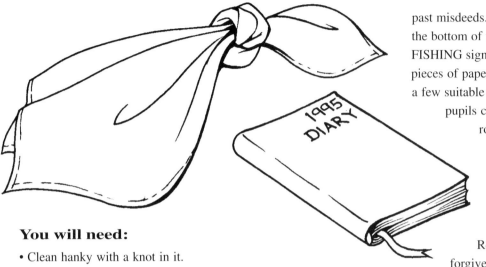

You will need:

- Clean hanky with a knot in it.
- Diary.
- A photocopy of the NO FISHING sign (provided).
- A bowl of water and a stone (optional).
- An improvised fishing rod (stick, string and magnet) (optional).
- Pieces of paper with paper clips on them. (optional)

Introduction

Talk about forgetting things and different ways of jogging your memory. Show the diary etc. Ask the pupils about different ways they have of remembering. There are some events it is right to remember and commemorate. There are other things about which it is better not to remind people.

Core Material

Read the Biblical Material and make it clear to pupils that this proverb is about the ordinary ups and downs of friendship. When someone makes a mistake, real friends don't keep reminding them of it. If people keep reminding others of the wrong they have done in the past it shows that they bear a grudge and have not forgiven them. People may find it hard to forget, but it is not necessary to keep dredging things up.

In the Bible, it talks about God putting people's wrongs behind his back or throwing them to the bottom of the sea (Isaiah 38.17, 43.25; Micah 7.18-19). These are word pictures: they mean God has forgiven people's wrongs and he is not going to keep reminding them of past misdeeds. It is as if he has put them at the bottom of the ocean and put up a NO FISHING sign. If you have the rod and pieces of paper, introduce them here. Write a few suitable wrongs on the papers and pupils can fish for them with the rod.

It does not help, either ourselves or others, if we keep dredging up past wrongs, whether that be our own or other people's. Remind the pupils that forgiveness does not mean putting up with ill-treatment.

Prayer/Reflection

Show the NO FISHING sign. If you have a bowl of water and a stone, ask the children to look at the sign and then close their eyes and listen for the splash as the stone sinks. The splash is a reminder of God's forgiveness. Read Micah 7.18-19: 'Who is as forgiving as God? He delights to show mercy and hurls our wrongs to the bottom of the ocean.' God forgives: it is as if he puts people's sins at the bottom of the sea and puts up a NO FISHING sign.

Father, help us to remember that you forgive. Give us the generosity do the same for others.

Note. For guidance on prayers and reflections see pages 9-11.

Never stop learning

Biblical Material: Proverbs: 4.13, 19.27

'Hold on to what you learn, for your education is your life.'

'When you stop learning, you soon neglect what you already know.'

You will need:

• A calculator.
• A sheet of paper and a thick felt-tipped pen.
• Some clean pebbles (optional).

Introduction

Talk with pupils about the length of time they spend in school. Using the calculator, pupils can calculate the minimum time spent in school in hours and write them up:

6 hours a day
5 days a week
39 weeks a year
11 years minimum

Core Material

Read the Biblical Material. Time spent in school is not the only time we learn. Most of a person's learning is done between 0-5 years. Talk with the pupils about the type of things we learn then. Learning goes on for ever. Teachers might like to talk with pupils about what people can learn during the following activities:

• Playing with friends and family, and leisure activities.
• TV/reading/eating etc.
• Time spent helping: tidying room, shopping etc.
• At Church/Sunday school.

In the Bible education is about a way of life. Christians believe God has filled the world with things to discover - about himself and the way he made the world. However long people live, they only ever find out a little about the world. The great scientist Isaac Newton, who discovered gravity, was a Christian. He said he felt like a small boy who had managed to pick up a few pebbles of knowledge from a vast beach. As a Christian, Newton felt that life was a journey of discovery and learning which never ended.

Prayer/Reflection

Ask pupils to close their eyes and imagine a vast beach full of pebbles. Some may have been on holiday to such a beach. Suggest that they imagine themselves bending down and picking up one pebble. Newton thought that each piece of knowledge was like picking up a pebble from a huge beach. Ask pupils to think quietly about things they have discovered or learnt.

Lord, you have crammed the world full of things to discover and learn. Teach us that the excitement of discovery never ends.

Note: if you have some clean pebbles pupils can write on them things they have learnt which excited them or made them full of wonder. A pebble display can become a focus for reflection.

Note. For guidance on prayers and reflections see pages 9-11.

Education and life

Biblical Material: Proverbs 27.17

'People learn from each other just as you use iron to sharpen iron.'

You will need:

• A knife sharpener (optional).
• A knife (make sure it is kept safely).
• A carrot to chop.
• A chopping board.

Introduction

Show the knife and sharpener (if available) and demonstrate it. Talk about how it works. Explain to children that knives get blunt after a while and need sharpening by rubbing against metal. Demonstrate the sharpness of the knife with the carrot.

Just as knives become sharper if rubbed against metal, so minds improve if they rub against other people's ideas.

Core Material

Read the Biblical Material. People learn from each other and that can improve their minds. Just as metal needs other metal to become sharp, so we need other people's ideas to help our own thinking. In the Bible, learning is not just learning facts such as 12 x 12 = 144. Ask pupils for more of this type of facts or use some of those listed.

Facts

• The capital of Mongolia is Ulaan Baator
• The largest diamond was found in 1905. It was as big as a man's fist.
• The Netherlands grow more flowers than any other country.
• India has the most languages in one country.

Education is not just what goes on in school. In the Bible, learning (education) is about relationships as well as facts, and it includes learning about God and his world. The word 'knowledge' in the Bible is used of the closest friendships. The idea of just collecting information would have seemed strange to people in Bible times. The whole purpose of education in the Bible was education for life - a life lived in friendship with God and others.

Prayer/Reflection

Ask the pupils to respond with 'We thank you, Heavenly Father,' after each line if appropriate, or listen quietly to the prayer.

For all we can learn about your world. 'We thank you, Heavenly Father'.

For knowledge we gain from books and television. 'We thank you, Heavenly Father'.

For knowledge we gain from sharing ideas with others. 'We thank you, Heavenly Father'.

For a world full of things to learn. 'We thank you, Heavenly Father'.

Note. For guidance on prayers and reflections see pages 9-11.

Worry

Biblical Material: Proverbs 12.25

'Worry can make you miserable and can rob you of happiness, but kind words can cheer the heart.'

You will need:

- A bicycle (optional).
- A bicycle lock (combination variety if possible).
- Any form of anti theft device (optional).

Introduction

If you can arrange to cycle (safely) into the assembly it makes a good start. If this is not possible, just show pupils the bicycle lock. See if one of them can work out the combination. Show the other anti theft devices: let the pupils try them. Explain how they work and talk about why we have them. What type of items might get stolen if locks are not used?

Core Material

Read the Biblical Material. Explain that worry is like a robber. Just as thieves might steal a bicycle if we do not lock it, so worry comes and robs people of happiness. Worry doesn't solve the problem, it just makes us unhappy. Jesus' advice was to take one day at a time and not to worry about the distant future. Worrying about the future spoils tomorrow and today. 'Each day has enough trouble of its own,' Jesus said. A poet called John Dryden put it like this: 'Tomorrow do your worst, for I have lived today.'

Jesus advised people to trust in God rather than worry. He did not promise a trouble-free life, but he did say that, whatever people faced, they would never have to face it alone. He said he would always be there: 'I will be with you always, even to the end of the world.' (Matthew 28. 20). We cannot alter tomorrow by worrying about it but we can make sure we make the most of today. Teachers may like to read, 'The Very Worried Sparrow' (Lion) to younger children.

Prayer/Reflection

Use the line of the Dryden poem as a recurring refrain after each of the following lines:

I have played with friends today. (refrain)
I have shown someone I cared today. (refrain)
I have laughed today. (refrain)
I have learnt something today. (refrain) etc.

Alternative

Pupils can look at the locks, then close their eyes while the prayer is said.

Tomorrow

Biblical Material: Proverbs 27.1

'Never boast about what is going to happen tomorrow. You don't know what will happen in between the time of your boasting and tomorrow arriving.'

You will need:

Several boxes gift wrapped and tied with ribbon: inside each should be something that can be heard when you rattle the parcel.

Introduction

Talk about waiting for Christmas, seeing the presents wrapped up and being tempted to take a look. Sometimes we might rattle or feel presents and try to guess their contents. Invite pupils to come up and rattle the presents and guess the contents. They can open the presents and see if they were correct.

Core Material

Read the Biblical Material. Christians believe that 'tomorrow' is like a present for which people have to wait. If people boast about what will happen, it shows they are not content to let tomorrow arrive like a surprise present. Some presents are a pleasant surprise, some are disappointing. If people knew what was about to happen, they would spend all their time dreading the future or looking forward to it, and never really enjoying today. Christians believe that each tomorrow is different and should be accepted on trust. A Christian called Dom Helder Camara wrote this:

Don't let yourself be torn
between yesterday
and tomorrow.
Live always and only
God's today.

Prayer/Reflection

Place the presents on the table and ask the pupils to think of the days ahead as presents as they listen to the prayer.

Lord, help us to accept surprises that upset our plans,
That reshape our days.
Forgive us when we try to control your tomorrow,
To predict what will happen,
To boast about it.
May each day dawn as a surprise present .

Note. For guidance on prayers and reflections see pages 9-11.

Hope

Biblical Material: Proverbs 13.12, 23.18.

'When you are disappointed and your hopes are dashed, the heart is crushed, but when a hope for the future comes true it fills you with joy.'

'There is surely a future hope for you which will not fail.'

You will need:

• A heart drawn on a paper bag with a smiling face drawn on the heart.
• A coin.
• A freezer tie.
• Paper and a thick felt-tipped pen.

Introduction

Ask the pupils to imagine they have been shipwrecked on a desert island. What would they need to live? List some of their suggestions.

One of the Biblical words for hope (used in Proverbs 23.18) originally meant 'backside' - not the thing we sit upon, more like the backside of the moon or the other side of a coin. It came to stand for the things we could not see: the future. When you look at a coin in your hand, you know the other side exists, even though you can't see it. Ask pupils to demonstrate this (allow them to see the coin first). Flip the coin and ask pupils to tell you what is on the side they cannot see. Hope is belief in what is certain yet unseen. For Christians it is the belief that good will triumph because it depends on God who does not fail.

> *Needs*
> Food
> House
> Drink
> Clothes

Core Material

People survive if they have food and water and some shelter, but it is only survival. To really live we need some 'invisibles'. Open the paper bag and ask the pupils to suggest some of the invisibles such as love and hope that people need to live. Write the 'invisibles' on pieces of paper and place them in the bag. When a hope is destroyed or crushed, people feel crushed inside (screw up the bag, crush it in your hands): but when a wish comes true people feel filled with joy. Blow up the bag and tie the bag with a freezer tie. Hope, like love, is not an optional extra, it is an essential of life - like water. Without hope and things to look forward to, life is bleak indeed.

Prayer/Reflection

Screw up the paper bag and read the verse, then blow it up again.

People are hungry, Lord, even though they have food: hungry for love, hungry for care, hungry for hope. It is not enough to survive: you have made us for more than that. We need love for today and hope for tomorrow.

Note. For guidance on prayers and reflections see pages 9-11.

Temptation

Biblical Material: Proverbs 1.10-19

'When bad people tempt you - don't give in. If they try to get you to join in the wrong they are doing, refuse. Stay away from them. People like that are only setting a trap for themselves. People who live by violence get hurt in the end.'

> God does not punish people for what they might have done

A Christian who lived in the twelfth century.

> I can resist anything but temptation

Anonymous

> Jesus was tempted just as we are but never did any wrong

The Bible

You will need:

- Two paper speech or thought bubbles.
- A large felt-tipped pen and paper.

Introduction

Talk about the sort of things people get tempted to do. When people are tempted, there is a battle going on inside. Imagine someone finding a purse full of money. One half of them might say, 'Go on, take it: no one will know.' The other might say, 'Find out who owns it.' Write these or other suggestions by the pupils in the bubbles. Pupils might like to turn this into an impromptu sketch. One pupil can be the person who finds the purse, two others can be the arguments for and against handing it in.

Core Material

Read the Biblical Material. This part of the Book of Proverbs advises people not to be tempted to join in violence. People who are violent or bully others are like a person digging a pit and then falling in it. Violence not only harms the victims, it also harms the people who are involved in it. There is nothing wrong with being tempted - everybody is tempted. The Bible says Jesus was tempted but didn't give in to it. It is giving in to temptation that is the problem, not temptation itself. Look at the sayings about temptation. Ask pupils what they mean.

Prayer/Reflection

Write TEMPT in large letters down the edge of a piece of paper. Write, then read, each sentence, line by line. In-between each sentence, ask pupils to reflect on its meaning.

Tempted: it's part of being human.

Everyone: it happens to everyone at any age - adults are tempted as well as children.

More: the Bible says temptation is not more than we can bear. With God's help we can resist.

Prayer: Christians ask God's help to resist when they pray.

Test: temptation tests us: we only know we really value truth when we are tempted to lie.

Encouraged: other people can encourage us to resist temptation.

Defeated: it can be defeated.

When we are tempted to join in wrong, Lord, give us the strength to resist.

Note. For guidance on prayers and reflections see pages 9-11.

A clear conscience

Biblical Material: Proverbs 20.9

'No one is perfect. Can anyone really say their conscience is completely clear?'

You will need:

• Labels saying 'hand' and 'arm' and 'conscience'.
• A bell.

Introduction

Ask pupils to apply just the hand and arm labels to you. Christians believe there is another part of us which is invisible. It is called a conscience. The conscience is not a part of the body like a hand, so we cannot put the label on any part of the body. Having a conscience is the ability to recognise the difference between right and wrong in our behaviour. It's almost like having a 'voice' or feeling inside. Part of the role of conscience is to act as a warning, like a fire bell. Ring the bell. It warns people of wrong behaviour.

Sometimes the conscience goes wrong, just as an alarm system could develop a fault if it wasn't checked regularly. Some people's conscience does not tell them that certain things are wrong. Christians believe this happens when the conscience is ignored too often. People become deaf to its 'voice' and no longer hear it.

Sometimes an alarm goes off even when there is no fire. A smoke alarm can be activated by burning the toast! In a similar way, some people have an over-active conscience. That means it keeps telling them they are doing things wrong when they aren't. If this happens, it needs checking out with other people you trust, just as you would check a smoke alarm.

Core Material

Read the Biblical Material. A clear conscience means the 'voice' inside is saying, 'You have done nothing wrong.' Nobody has a really clear conscience: everybody has done something wrong at some time.

Once Jesus was teaching when people dragged before him a woman who had broken the law. The accusers were pleased with themselves: she had been caught 'red handed'. All Jesus had to do was pass sentence and condemn her. After that, they would throw stones at the woman in order to kill her. Jesus quietly drew in the dirt with his finger, and said, 'Anyone who has never done wrong can throw the first stone.' Then he continued writing on the ground with his finger. The people put down their stones and went home. No one had a clear conscience. Every person was reminded, by their conscience, of the wrongs they had done. When Jesus eventually looked up, he asked the woman where everyone was. 'Is there no one to condemn you?' asked Jesus. 'None,' said the woman. 'I don't condemn you either,' Jesus replied. 'Go home, but don't sin again.' (John 8.1-11).

Knowing we all do wrong is not depressing: it can make us gentle in our treatment of others. It does not mean we have to accept wrong. Jesus told the woman to stop sinning.

Prayer/Reflection

Ask the pupils to sit quietly and listen while you ring the bell.

(Sound the bell quietly) *When conscience whispers, help us to listen with care.*

(Sound the bell loudly) *When conscience shouts too often, may we listen but check.*

Whether it shouts or whispers, help us, God, never to ignore your warning system.

Note. For guidance on prayers and reflections see pages 9-11.

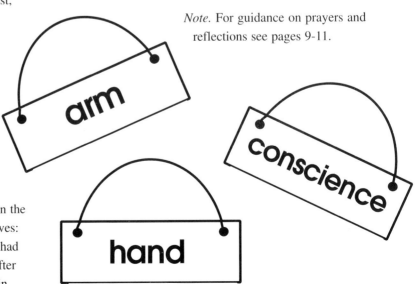

Warnings

Biblical Material: Proverbs 25.12

'A warning given by an experienced and trustworthy person to those who are willing to listen is more valuable than gold.'

You will need:

- A motorist's warning triangle or similar device.
- Several red paper triangles each with a hole punched in the top.
- A wire coat hanger.
- Some wool to hang up the triangles.
- Scissors.

Introduction

Set up the triangle and explain its use: where it is placed, and the warning it gives to other motorists. Talk with the pupils about warning signals such as light houses, flashing lights etc. Ask for suggestions as to other warning devices.

Core Material

A warning triangle tells the motorist, in advance, that there is trouble ahead: another motorist has broken down. A warning triangle stops one car colliding with another. Sometimes warnings come from other people, who can see us heading for trouble, and who care enough to warn us. Read the Biblical Material. The Bible adds two conditions concerning warnings by other people:

- it should be from an experienced person, someone who has seen this sort of thing before.

- the person asking for advice should listen.

Some warnings fall on deaf ears and are wasted, just as some motorists see fog warnings on the motor way and ignore them. Giving warnings is part of being a responsible friend, but it does not always make you popular. If the friendship is a good one, it will be able to survive those occasions when warnings are needed. Jesus was not afraid of warning people if he saw that what they were doing was wrong. Once Jesus warned his followers about the dangers of wealth with these words: 'It is easier for a camel to go through the eye of a needle than for a rich man to go to heaven.' (Mark 10.25).

He did not mean rich people could not go to heaven. He was warning that sometimes riches make it hard because wealth becomes all important.

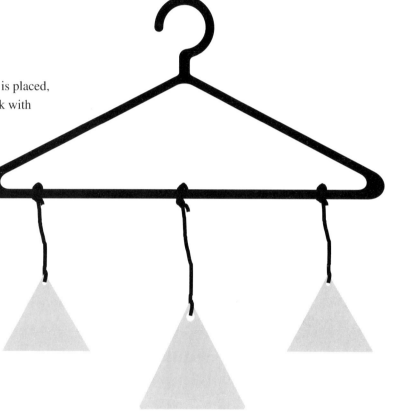

Prayer/Reflection

A warning mobile.

Take a wire coat hanger and hang it up. Ask several pupils to thread the wool through the paper triangles. Ask the pupils for suggestions of things a friend might warn another not to do because it will lead to danger and trouble. Write the suggestions on the triangles and hang them on the coat hanger as a mobile. The suggestions can then become the focus for prayer or reflection.

Note. For guidance on prayers and reflections see pages 9-11.

Look in your heart

Biblical Material: Proverbs 27.19

'If you look in the water, you see your face reflected back at you. If you look in your heart, it reflects your own self.'

You will need:

- A mirror.
- A large felt-tipped pen.
- A sheet of aluminium foil.
- Some Sticky-Tack. (reusable adhesive).
- Paper.

Introduction

Choose a few people (choose sensitively) to look into the mirror and describe what they see. Talk about reflection. If a mirror could reflect what people were thinking and feeling inside, would it sell? Create an instant advert for such a mirror, using pupil suggestions.

Core Material

Read the poem below. Explain that there is no special mirror on the market that reveals what people are like on the inside, It is not needed. People are quite capable of looking at themselves - not their looks, but their behaviour and the type of person they are. The Bible describes this as 'looking in your heart.' The writer of this poem, Edgar Guest, talks about looking at himself but it is not his face he is concerned with, but what he is like as a person.

Myself

I have to live with myself, and so
I want to be fit for myself to know.
I want to be able as days go by
Always to look myself straight in the eye.
I don't want to stand with the setting sun
And hate myself for the things I've done.

Read the Biblical Material. If people look inside themselves - not with their eyes but with their minds- they see the type of person they are. Explain this so that there are no misunderstandings. Everyone will see things they do not like: no one is perfect. These things need dealing with, because they may spoil our lives or the lives of others. Christians believe people also have to answer to God for what they have done with their lives.

Prayer/ Reflection

Roll out a length of aluminium foil on a table and write on the 'mirror' you have created some of the good and bad things people might 'see' if they look inside their hearts - keep this impersonal. Hold it up and read the prayer while pupils look at the 'mirror'.

Heavenly Father, we have wronged you and others:
in the things we have thought,
the words we have said
and the things we have done.
We are sorry and want to change.

Note. For guidance on prayers and reflections see pages 9-11.

Self control

Biblical Material: Proverbs 16.32

'A patient person is better than a soldier, and it is better to win control over yourself than win control of whole cities.'

You will need:

• A radio controlled car (optional).
• A bowl.
• A packet of corn flakes.

Introduction

Bring in the radio controlled car and show the pupils how it works. It is controlled from the outside. You can make it go where you wish. It is the same with robots. They are controlled by a computer programme. They can't think for themselves. You can demonstrate this by using a pupil or another member of staff to act as a robot. Stand the person in front of a table and treat them as a robot. Give them instructions on opening a packet of corn flakes and pouring them in the bowl. They must not think for themselves.

Example: Lift the packet. Stop.
Move hand to the right. Stop.
Tilt the packet. Stop.

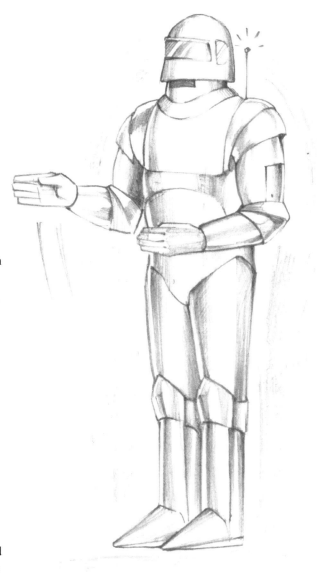

Core Material

Read the Biblical Material. Self control is when you don't need someone else to make you do things. Radio controlled cars and robots need other people to control or programme them. Christians believe God has not made people like robots. People are free to make their own decisions about right and wrong. People are free to ask for advice or help from God or others, but in the end it is up to them what they do. That freedom includes the freedom to do wrong, although there are consequences which have to be taken into account. Some wrong doing, such as stealing, is against the law. If people choose this type of wrong, they get in trouble with the law. Other types of wrong doing, such as lying, are not generally against the law but they do have consequences in people's lives.

Prayer/Reflection

After you have read the prayer below, ask the pupils to think what the 'prayer of the robot' might be. Would it wish for freedom, or is freedom too much of a responsibility?

I wish I was a robot,
With a chip for a heart
And a computer for a brain.
Being a robot is easy,
You don't have to think -
Just follow your programme.
Being human is difficult,
You have to make choices.
Help us, Father, to control ourselves
And make right choices with your help.

Note. For guidance on prayers and reflections see pages 9-11.

Sincerity

Biblical Material: Proverbs 26.23

'Some people use words to hide what they are really thinking. Such talk is like an expensive glaze on a cheap pot.'

You will need:

- A clay pot without a glaze on it.
- A good pot with a fine glaze.
- Some paper cut as speech and thought bubbles.
- A thick felt-tipped pen.

Introduction

Show the two pots and ask the pupils to explain the difference. Explain what a glaze is. Glaze covers the cheap material the pot is made from. It makes it look good.

Core Material

Read the Biblical Material. Insincerity is when fine words are used to cover bad thoughts or actions, just as glaze covers clay. It is when when thoughts don't match words or actions. It would be insincere if someone said they liked you but inside were thinking horrible thoughts about you. Ask pupils to suggest some ways of being insincere, using thought and speech bubbles.

Jesus said insincere people were like cups which had been washed on the outside but were still dirty on the inside (Matthew 23. 25-26). Some people sound good when they talk but are horrible inside. The Bible says that people should match their thoughts, their words and their actions so that others know what they are really like.

Prayer/Reflection

Stand the two bowls on a table. Read the Biblical Material again. Read the prayer below.

Life can be a matching game - thoughts matching words, words matching actions.
Help us, Father, to be sincere in all we think, say and do. May we never use fine words to cover selfish and unkind thoughts.

Note. For guidance on prayers and reflections see pages 9-11.

Motives

Biblical Material: Proverbs 16. 2

'People may think everything they do is right, but the Lord judges not only the actions but also the motives.'

You will need:

- A range of items, of differing values.
- A charity collection tin, (home-made) or collecting plate.
- Ten coins (any denomination).
- A £5 pound note, a 1p coin.

Introduction

Ask the pupils what £5 could buy. Ask them what 1p would buy. Give one pupil a £5 note and another 1p. Ask them to come and select items they could buy for either £5 or 1p. Talk with the pupils about the difference between the two amounts. If both were put in a collection box, which would be the greater amount? This story is about a woman who gave very little, but Jesus said it was considered a great amount by God owing to her motives and circumstances.

Core Material

Tell the story of the widow's mite. This can be found in Luke 21.1-4.

In the Temple at Jerusalem stood large collection boxes into which people dropped their donations as they went by. As Jesus watched, some rich people went by, dropping in huge amounts. Later, a very poor widow crept by. She dropped in two tiny copper coins. Together the coins were worth far less than 1p. Jesus turned to his disciples and said, 'That poor widow gave far more than all the others: they gave and still had plenty left over. She gave her all.'

Talk with the pupils about the giving in this story. Read the Biblical Material. The widow was different from the others who gave large amounts because her circumstances were different. She was unlikely to be showing off in her giving, when she was so desperately poor. She was not giving her 'left over' money. Her motives must have been very strong to give everything she had. In the Bible, it constantly emphasises that God looks at motives behind giving, not the gift itself.

Prayer/Reflection

Ask some pupils to drop a few coins into the collection tin/plate before each line.

(Drop coins) ***Some give because they feel they have to.***
(Drop coins) ***Some give because they want to show off.***
(Drop coins) ***Some give because they have lots of spare money.***
(Drop coins) ***Some give because they feel guilty.***
(Drop coins) ***Some give because they care.***

Note. For guidance on prayers and reflections see pages 9-11.

Friends and enemies

Biblical Material: Proverbs 27.6

'Better the blow of a friend than the kiss of an enemy.

You will need:

• A large sheet of paper.
• A large felt-tipped pen.

Introduction

Write up some simple maths problems and deliberately put in the wrong answer. Ask the pupils to correct your work. Do the same with some spelling. It is not pleasant getting back work with corrections on it. It can be upsetting to see our mistakes corrected.

Core Material

People need their mistakes correcting in order to learn. It is the same in life. People who care about their friends, correct them when they go wrong. It might be an unpleasant experience but it can help people to change. It is easy to think that true friends are those who say nice things, and dismiss people who point out mistakes as enemies. The Bible calls criticism by someone who cares for us 'the blow of a friend,' because criticism by a friend can feel like a slap in the face. It is not advising people to hit each other!

The opposite of 'the blow of a friend,' is 'the kiss of an enemy'. Kissing was the way people greeted each other in Biblical times. It was an outward sign of friendship. Some people pretend to be friends, have all the outward show, say all the right things but don't really care. Jesus had a friend called Judas who eventually betrayed him to his enemies. You can find this story in Mark 14.43-50. Judas betrayed Jesus with a kiss, the normal greeting of a friend. (See the drawing on page 82). He had the outward show of friendship but no more.

Prayer/Reflection

Show the picture of Judas' betrayal (it can be enlarged or copied onto an acetate). Judas is about to kiss Jesus. The artist has caught the moment just before it happens. Judas still has a few seconds to make his choice.

The example of Judas stands as a warning that the outward show of friendship is not always the real thing. Give us the judgement not to reject our friends when they risk telling us we are making a mistake. What feels like a slap in the face might be real friendship.

Note. For guidance on prayers and reflections see pages 9-11.

Growing up

Biblical Material: Proverbs 12.1

'People who want to grow in knowledge want to be told when they are wrong. Hating correction is stupid.'

You will need:

• A clean toy watering can/plastic bottle filled with water.
• A list of ingredients on the back of the bottle/can as in the drawing.
• A plant.
• A picture of a baby.

Introduction

Talk about the way we grow and change as we get older. One way of measuring growth is to measure height, another is to measure weight. Emphasise that we all grow at different rates. Show the picture of the baby. Talk about how much they weighed as babies and how much they have grown. Do not compare children with each other.

Core Material

People do not only grow in their bodies, they grow inside too, in their minds and personalities. This is difficult to measure. You cannot weigh this type of growth or measure it with a metre stick. You have to look for signs of it. One of the signs of growing inside is when people can accept being told they are wrong. This is extremely difficult to accept because it hurts our pride, but there is no growth without it. Growing up is not only a matter of age, it is a matter of attitude. Some children are very grown up in their attitudes.

Ask pupils what plants need to grow. Just as plants need water, sun and soil to grow, so human minds and hearts need a number of things to grow: love, security and helpful criticism.

Show pupils the bottle/can and tell them it's a special formula that makes people grow. Ask a pupil to read the ingredients. Pupils might like to add some extra ingredients to the list.

Read the Biblical Material and explain how helpful criticism can help people to grow. Explain afterwards that it is only water in the can.

Prayer/Reflection

Three pupils can take it in turns to water the plant, saying a line each, if appropriate.

Like seeds in need of warmth and soil, we need a watering of love.
Like plants in need of sun and rain, we need a watering of care.
Like plants in need of heat and shade, we need a watering of help when we go wrong.

Note. For guidance on prayers and reflections see pages 9-11.

God's warning system

Biblical Material: Proverbs 18.3

'Sin and shame go together.'

You will need:

- A number of 'pairs'- salt and pepper etc.
- Paper
- A thick felt-tipped pen.

Introduction

Show the pupils your pairs of items: alternatively, mix
the items and ask pupils to sort them into pairs for you.
Ask the pupils to suggest other pairs: Laurel and Hardy,
Batman and Robin etc. List these on the sheet of paper

> Batman and Robin
> fish and chips
> salt and pepper

Prayer/Reflection

A group of pupils can say the following prayer taking
one line each.

Like Batman and Robin
Fish and chips
Rhubarb and custard
Salt and pepper
Sin and shame belong together.
Help us, Father, never to separate them.

Note. For guidance on prayers and reflections see
pages 9-11.

Core Material

Read the Biblical Material. The Bible suggests
two things that should go together sin (or wrong)
and shame. Explain what being ashamed is. The
reason they should go together is because
Christians believe shame is God's warning
mechanism, like pain. Just as pain tells people
to stop doing something that is hurting, or to
get help, so shame is unpleasant and tells
people to stop doing wrong. Shame,
however, should only go with things that
are really wrong such as lying and
stealing. Pain is unpleasant - but it keeps
people safe. Shame is unpleasant, but it
keeps people safe from wrong.

Sometimes people feel a slight
twinge of pain and there is nothing
really wrong but it needs checking
all the same. In a similar way,
people sometimes feel shame or
guilt when they haven't done
anything wrong. The warning
system has gone slightly wrong.
If this happens, check it out:
if you haven't done anything
wrong, it's a false alarm.

Seven things God does not tolerate

Biblical Material: Proverbs 6.16-19

'There are seven things which God does not tolerate: a proud look, a lying tongue, hands that shed innocent blood, a mind that thinks up evil plans, feet that rush to do evil, a witness who tells lies, and a person who stirs up trouble among friends.'

You will need:

- Three strips of red paper.
- Glue stick.
- Paper and a thick felt-tipped pen.
- Sticky-Tack (reusable adhesive).

Introduction

Talk with pupils about the things you can't stand - for example, music in supermarkets or whatever your pet hate is. Keep it fairly light-hearted. The pupils might like to share some of their pet hates.

> ### Pet hates
>
> Music in supermarkets
> Cardboard milk cartons
> People who talk through films

Core Material

All the pet hates talked about are petty. The Bible talks about seven things which God does not like. These are not little things, such as music in supermarkets, but serious things such as violence and stealing. Read the Biblical Material. Normally people are told to be tolerant but it is never suggested that they tolerate wrong. Talk with the pupils about the type of behaviour that is not tolerated in school. Explain that during the next seven assemblies they will be looking at some of the seven things the Bible says God does

not tolerate. See if they can name all seven from the reading. Make a list and ask what they all have in common. They are all things which wreck a community, that make living together impossible. Explain that each day you will look at one of the things on the list. Each day a red warning triangle will go up and a different picture will be inside each triangle. The red triangle warns of danger, as a motorist's red triangle warns of a breakdown ahead. These seven things are dangerous because each one hurts others and ourselves.

Prayer/Reflection

Invite several pupils to help you glue the three strips into a triangle and put them on the wall. Ask the pupils to sit in silence for a moment and quietly think about one thing from the list and the damage it can cause.

Note. For guidance on prayers and reflections see pages 9-11.

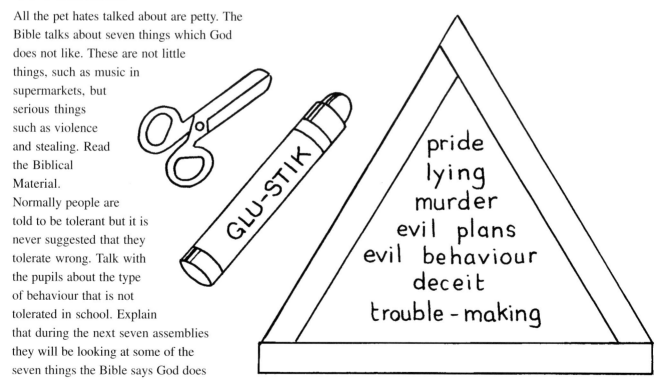

pride
lying
murder
evil plans
evil behaviour
deceit
trouble - making

Seven things God does not tolerate: a proud look

Biblical Material: Proverbs 6.16-19

Read all the verses (page 69). This assembly focuses on, 'A proud look.' Proverbs 6.17.

You will need:

- A proud face (provided).
- Three strips of red paper.
- Glue stick .
- Sticky-Tack (reusable adhesive).
- A thick felt-tipped pen.
- Scissors.
- Paper.

Introduction

Show the pupils the proud face. Ask them what the expression suggests to them. They might like to create a speech bubble to go with the face. Ask what someone wearing this expression might be saying or thinking, and write their suggestions in the bubble.

Core Material

Read the Biblical Material. There are two types of pride. One type is good: it is looking at something you have done and being proud of the achievement. The other type is when people look down on everyone else and boast about how great they are by comparison. This sort of pride is destructive: it destroys people's self confidence. God doesn't tolerate the wrong type of pride because it hurts other people. Christians believe God created everyone. Therefore he feels hurt if one of the people he created is made to feel small or useless.

Prayer/ Reflection

Pupils can make a red triangle as before and place it on the wall. Place the face inside it. Write 'pride' underneath the face. Ask pupils to think quietly about the wrong type of pride. End with the prayer below.

Pride is dangerous.
Pride is a weapon we use on other people,
It cuts them down to size.
Pride is like a pair of glasses that magnifies the way we see ourselves
And makes others seem smaller.
Give us the humility, Father, to see ourselves as you do-
Full of potential, not perfect, but created and loved by you.

Note. For guidance on prayers and reflections see pages 9-11.

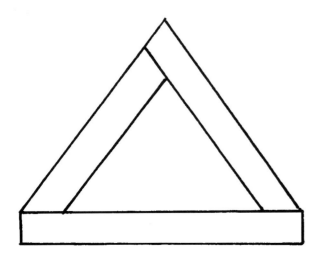

Seven things God does not tolerate: a lying tongue

Biblical Material: Proverbs 6.16-19

Read all the verses (page 69).This assembly focuses on, 'A lying tongue' Proverbs 6.17.

You will need:

- A glass of water lightly coloured with blackcurrant drink.
- Three strips of red paper.
- Glue stick.
- Sticky-Tack (reusable adhesive)
- A thick felt-tipped pen.
- Scissors.
- Paper.

Introduction

Talk with pupils about the difficulty of not knowing when someone is telling the truth. People do not have an in-built system warning others when they are not telling the truth. It would be a lot easier if someone's eyes flashed red or their hair stood on end every time they told a lie, then people would know whether to trust them or not.

Core Material

Show your drink. Ask the pupils to imagine you are a scientist who has just invented a new truth drink. One swallow and the person who has drunk it just has to tell the truth. Ask the pupils how they would advertise the drink. Use their suggestions to create an instant advert.

Ask pupils to list the advantages of people telling the truth. What are the disadvantages? The Bible's advice is to, 'Speak the truth in love.' (Ephesians 4. 25). In other words, 'Tell the truth but with tact and gentleness.' Read the Biblical Material. It says God does not tolerate lies. It is right not to tolerate some things: lying is one of them: it destroys friendship and causes trouble.

Telling the truth is never easy: it is occasionally dangerous. People have died because they told the truth about evil governments. Archbishop Romero of El Salvador in Central America was shot because he would not keep quiet about the evil he saw around him. Most of us don't face this type of situation, but we all need courage in our own situations to speak the truth, and wisdom to know how to do that safely.

Prayer/Reflection

Pupils can make a red triangle as before. Draw a tongue on a piece of paper and place it inside the triangle. Write 'lies' underneath. Ask pupils to think about the courage it takes to tell the truth.

Father, we pray today for all those who have the courage to speak the truth in difficult situations. We remember people such as Archbishop Romero who died because he dared to speak the truth about the evil around him. In our own situations, give us the courage to speak the truth in love.

Note. For guidance on prayers and reflections see pages 9-11.

Seven things God does not tolerate: hands that shed innocent blood

Biblical Material: Proverbs 6.16-19

Read all the verses quoted on page 69. This assembly focuses on 'Hands that shed innocent blood.' Proverbs 6.17.

You will need:

- Paper.
- A thick felt-tipped pen.
- Glue stick.
- Scissors.
- Three strips of red paper.
- Sticky-Tack (reusable adhesive).
- Newspaper clippings (optional).
- A candle and matches (optional).
- A tray of damp sand (optional).

Introduction

Draw round a pupil's hands on a piece of paper. Ask the other pupils to suggest the type of things which hands can do, good and bad. Put the suggestions for good actions in or around one hand. Write the suggestions for bad actions in or around the other.

Core Material

Read the Biblical Material. Every day, in the news, we hear of the wrong in the world - stealing, violence, even murder. We seldom hear of the good things. They don't make the news. Maybe that is a good thing: maybe it means that these bad things are still rare enough to make the headlines. We need to remember that, if ever we feel overwhelmed by the bad news. We also need to know it is all right not to tolerate these things. Every time someone is hurt, it is not just another person: Christians believe it is someone God knew by name, someone he loved and created. There is no such thing as an unimportant person to God. Each person's hurt matters.

Prayer/Reflection

Pupils can make the red triangle as before. Draw round a pupil's hand and place inside the triangle. Write on the hand the word 'violence'.

Choose one or two items of news - choose sensitively. Ask the pupils to think/pray silently while you read the headlines and list people who need praying for. If you have a spare display board, some newspaper clippings can be pinned up and a candle lit before it. Place the candle in damp sand well away from the paper. Blow it out at the end of the prayer time. The 'prayer board' can become a regular feature of assemblies.

Note. For guidance on prayers and reflections see pages 9-11.

Seven things God does not tolerate: evil plans

Biblical Material: Proverbs 6.16-19

Read all the verses (page 69). This assembly focuses on 'A mind that thinks up evil plans.' Proverbs 6.18.

You will need:

- Sticky-Tack (reusable adhesive).
- Glue stick.
- Three strips of red paper .
- Scissors.
- Paper.
- Large felt tipped-pen.

plan unpleasant ones. They think up evil plans and ways to put them into action. There is a story in the Bible about a queen who thought up an evil plan. Jezebel was the Queen of Israel - her husband Ahab was the King. Ahab already had a palace garden, but he wanted to buy the garden of the person who lived next door, a man called Naboth. Naboth, however, said, 'No.' Ahab went home and sulked, but Jezebel started planning. She wrote her husband's signature on a document which told the rulers of Naboth's village to invite Naboth to a feast, and, while he was there, to accuse him of something he had not done. The rulers were to produce false witnesses, Naboth was to be found guilty and executed. Jezebel had her way. People were too frightened of her to disobey, but God noticed. Ahab and Jezebel's evil plan did them no good in the end. They got the extra garden but lost the throne.
(1 Kings 21).

Evil plans may in the short term succeed, but Christians believe God is a God of justice and that in the end such plans will fail.

Introduction

Talk about places where you do your best thinking. Some people do their best thinking late at night. A famous Greek thinker once solved a problem in the bath. It is said he jumped out shouting, 'Eureka!' (I've found it!). Draw a thought bubble and ask pupils where they do their best thinking. Put some of their suggestions in the bubble.

Core Material

Read the Biblical Material. Many significant actions are the result of previous planning and thinking. Just as you might plan a nice surprise in advance, so some people

Prayer/Reflection

Pupils can make a red triangle as before. Make a thought bubble that will fit in the triangle. Inside the bubble write 'evil plans'. Ask pupils to think about the trouble caused by plotting evil plans.

Thank you, God, that you are Judge as well as Father, that you judge evil plans and make sure they never triumph in the long run.

Note. For guidance on prayers and reflections see pages 9-11.

Seven things God does not tolerate: feet that rush to do evil

Biblical Material: Proverbs 6.16-19

Read all the verses (page 69). This assembly focuses on 'Feet that rush do evil.' Proverbs 6.18.

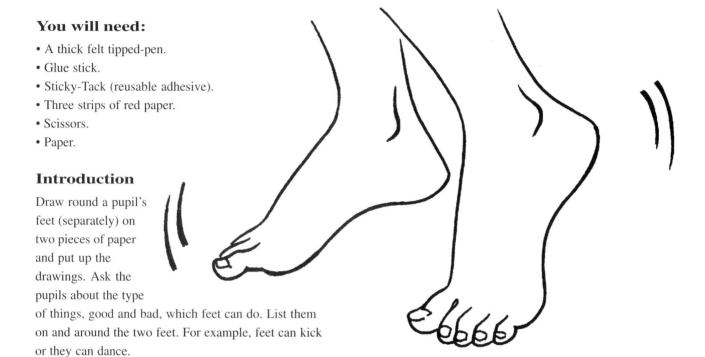

You will need:

• A thick felt tipped-pen.
• Glue stick.
• Sticky-Tack (reusable adhesive).
• Three strips of red paper.
• Scissors.
• Paper.

Introduction

Draw round a pupil's feet (separately) on two pieces of paper and put up the drawings. Ask the pupils about the type of things, good and bad, which feet can do. List them on and around the two feet. For example, feet can kick or they can dance.

Core Material

Read the Biblical Material. Feet do not have a life of their own. They are connected by nerves to our brains: our brains send messages according to what we think and feel. Ask some pupils to demonstrate. They can send the message to their feet asking them to jump, tap, skip, run etc. If we want to control what our feet do, we have to watch how we think, for our minds control our

bodies. If our feet do something bad (quote some of the things from the list), it is no good blaming them, as if they had a life of their own: the fault lies in ourselves. Christians believe people have been created with a mind and a conscience so that they can take responsibility for their actions.

Prayer/Reflection

Make the red triangle as before. Draw round a pupil's foot or use the one you have already drawn. Cut it out and place it in the triangle. Ask the pupils to think quietly about the results for the victims of evil actions. Write 'evil actions' on the foot.

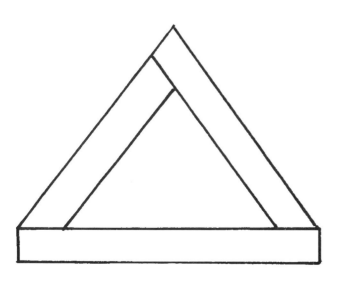

Feet to run, feet to hurt,
Feet to crush, feet to dance,
Feet to celebrate your world,
Feet to destroy.
For the billions of feet that walk your world,
We pray that they may dance and not destroy.

Note. For guidance on prayers and reflections see pages 9-11.

Seven things God does not tolerate: witnesses who lie

Biblical Material: Proverbs 6. 16-19.

Read all the verses quoted on page 69. This assembly focuses on 'Witnesses who lie.' Proverbs 6.19.

You will need:

• Packaging used for fragile items.
• Sticky-Tack (reusable adhesive).
• Glue stick.
• Three strips of red paper.
• An egg (hard boiled).
• A number of safe but fragile items.
• A picture of a hand on a Bible (provided).
• A thick felt-tipped pen.

Introduction

Talk about holding something fragile in your hand. Show your fragile items and demonstrate how you would package them, using pupils to help. Pupils could try walking across the room holding the egg (do not tell them it is hard boiled). Ask them about how it felt and how they carried it to keep it safe.

Core Material

Read the Biblical Material. Eggs are not the only fragile things in life. People are fragile too - not just their bodies, but their feelings and reputation. When you are a witness in a court of law, it is like holding a person's life in your hand: how that person is judged by others depends on what you say. Telling the truth in that situation becomes extremely important. In court, witnesses promise on the Bible that they will tell the truth. If people lie in court, it is treated as a crime, called perjury, because the truth is so important in that situation. We may not all be witnesses in court, but we often have to act as witnesses to accidents, fights, etc. Christians believe it is essential the truth is told on these occasions, not only because what happens to someone else depends on it, but because that person is known and loved by God. Lies can affect what happens to a person. Lies can wreck their reputation and hurt their feelings.

Prayer/Reflection

Pupils can make the red triangle as before. Show the picture of the hand on the Bible and place it inside the triangle. Write 'perjury' underneath. Explain that witnesses take an oath in court. Ask pupils to close their eyes and listen to the oath.

'I promise that the evidence that I shall give shall be the truth, the whole truth and nothing but the truth.'

Ask pupils to imagine they are holding an egg in their hand.

It takes very little to break an egg. It takes very little to get someone in trouble. Sometimes one lie will do it.

Note. For guidance on prayers and reflections see pages 9-11.

God does not tolerate:
a person who stirs up trouble among friends

Biblical Material: Proverbs 6.16-19.

Read all the verses (page 69). This assembly focuses on 'A person who stirs up trouble among friends.' Proverbs 6.19.

You will need:

• Three strips of red paper.
• Sticky-Tack (Reusable adhesive).
• A variety of wooden spoons.
• A large felt-tipped pen.
• Glue stick.
• Scissors.
• Paper.

Introduction

Talk about the job of a wooden spoon. Show the different varieties and ask the pupils what they could be used for:

a) long handled spoon for deep pans.
b) spoons with holes in for jam.
c) flat edged spoons for scraping the bottom of pans.
d) spoons with a point for getting into corners.

Core Material

All the wooden spoons have one thing in common - they are for stirring. Some people are like wooden spoons: they love to stir up trouble amongst friends. Read the Biblical Material. You may like to draw faces on a couple of spoons and use them as puppets. People who behave as wooden spoons whisper one thing to one person and tell a different story to someone

else, then stand back and watch the trouble they have stirred up. One person can cause a fight between two friends in this way. It is the people who fight who end up in trouble, although it is the 'stirrer' who was really the cause of the problem. What for some people is thoughtless fun causes other people hurt and trouble.

Prayer/Reflection

Pupils can make a red triangle as before. Draw a wooden spoon on a piece of paper or photocopy the one provided and place it inside the triangle. Write 'Stirrers' underneath.

Father forgive us when we stir instead of making peace. May we never be wooden spoons to our friends. Help us to remember that everyone is precious to you and should never be used as part of a harmful game.

Note. For guidance on prayers and reflections see pages 9-11.

Ears to hear

Biblical Material: Proverbs 20.12

'God created ears for listening.'

You will need:

- Sticky-Tack (reusable adhesive).
- Objects that make interesting sounds.
- A large cardboard box to place them in.
- Paper and a thick felt-tipped pen.

Introduction

Place the objects in the large box. Ask pupils to come and choose an object and create a noise with it inside the box. The other pupils can guess what object it is. Go through all the objects this way. Write the noises the objects make on paper. Pupils might like to suggest other sound words. *Note:* Use this assembly sensitively, particularly when hearing impaired children are present.

Core Material

Read the Biblical Material. Talk about the way the world is full of interesting noises. Christians believe God created the world full of sound for people to enjoy. He could have created just a few bird songs, just a few notes. Instead, Christians believe, he created a world full of a variety of sounds which should never be taken for granted. Talk with pupils about their favourite sounds, the ones they would miss if the world had been made silent.

Prayer/Reflection

Make an 'instant' poem or prayer in the assembly using the pupils' suggestions. Write the line, 'For the sound of...,' add some pupils' suggestions, and close their verse with the refrain, 'We thank you, Lord.' Repeat this with more suggestions by the pupils.

For the sound of -
Crisps crackling in a bag
The hiss of pop
The crunch of apples
We thank you, Lord.

An alternative idea is to use the sound words already written to create a prayer such as the one below.

Rattle, clatter, hiss,
Grate, growl, fizz,
Whisper, sizzle, crash,
Hum, sing, splash.
For your noisy, wonderful world, we thank you God.

Note. For guidance on prayers and reflections see pages 9-11.

Eyes to see

Biblical Material: Proverbs 20.12

'The Lord has given us eyes to see.'

You will need:

- A number of objects, which have interesting shapes, colours etc.
- A large cardboard box.

Introduction

Please handle sensitively if visually impaired children are present. Play a game of 'I spy' with pupils, using a wide variety of objects. Ask several pupils to come and look into the cardboard box and describe an item each. See if the other pupils can guess the objects correctly.

Core Material

Bring out the objects and put them on display. Ask pupils for their favourite 'sights': the five most favourite things they would miss if they no longer existed. Read the Biblical Material. Christians believe that God has filled the world with things for us to see. He could have made it dull and boring. He could have made the world full of square objects instead of lots of interesting shapes. Imagine a square sun and rectangular mountains! Talk with the pupils about the variety of shapes we have in our world.

We also have millions of colours and a variety of shades to enjoy. Computers can work in nearly seventeen million colours! Christians believe in an extravagant God. How often do people notice the colours in the world and stop to say thank you? With younger pupils, you might like to read 'The Day it Rained Colours' (Lion) or 'The Secret of the Rainbow' (Scripture Union). This assembly can be broadened into a 'rainbow' where the different colours of God's creation are celebrated daily. The seven assemblies which follow create the rainbow.

Prayer/Reflection

Ask pupils to think of the variety of colours with their eyes shut while listening to the prayer.

For red and purple,
Brown and green,
All the colours to be seen,
We thank you, Lord.

For blue of sky,
Gold of sun,
All your colours, every one,
We thank you, Lord.

Note. For guidance on prayers and reflections see pages 9-11.

Red

Biblical Material: Proverbs 20.12

These assemblies are a development of the assembly on page 79. They celebrate the colours which Christians believe God put into the world.

God created many different reds. Long ago, Christian painters used red as the colour of bravery: it was used to paint people who died for their beliefs. Write 'Thank you, God, for red,' on the strip of paper and place it on the wall. This creates the first strip of the rainbow.

> Thank you, God, for red

Prayer/Reflection

Place the red candle in the sand and light it. Pupils can think of different reds while the prayer is read.

For scarlet, blood and cherry red,
We thank you, Heavenly Father.
For crimson, fire and berry red,
We thank you, Heavenly Father.
For all the reds of earth and air,
Sunrise and sunset,
For all red colours everywhere,
We thank you, Heavenly
Father.

Note. For guidance on prayers and reflections see pages 9-11.

A rainbow of coloured candles can be created. They should always be placed in damp sand. Remember to extinguish the candles. Make sure all items brought in are safe.

You will need:

- A variety of red articles.
- A strip of red paper.
- A large felt-tipped pen.
- Sticky-Tack (reusable adhesive).
- Matches (optional).
- A red candle (optional).
- A tray of damp sand (optional).

Introduction

Ask the pupils to bring in some red items and describe them. They might be bright scarlet or deep maroon, rich cherry or holly-berry red. Place the items on the display table and talk about the variety of reds. Play colour 'I Spy' with pupils. 'I spy with my little eye something red beginning with ...'

Core Material

Christians believe God created the world to be an interesting place, full of variety. He could have created just one red, but then blood, roses, cherries, and strawberries would all look exactly the same. Instead,

Orange

Biblical Material: Proverbs 20.12

These assemblies are a development of the assembly on page 79. They celebrate the colours which Christians believe God put into the world.

You will need:

- A variety of orange articles.
- An orange.
- A strip of orange paper.
- A large felt-tipped pen.
- Sticky-Tack (reusable adhesive).
- An orange candle (optional).
- Matches (optional).
- A tray of damp sand (optional).

Introduction

Show the orange and talk about its colour. Ask the pupils to bring in some orange items and describe them. They might be hot fiery orange, tangerine, pale peach or deep burnt orange. Talk about orange as a colour. Is it a sad colour or a happy colour? What mood is orange?

Core Material

Brian Keenan was an Irishman working in Beirut (Lebanon) who was kidnapped. Brian spent the next four and a half years in dark, colourless prison cells, often underground. Food was adequate but boring. Brian Keenan tells of how, one day, he was given a bowl of fruit and amongst the fruit was an orange. Instead of eating the orange, Brian looked at it. He had been deprived of colour and sunlight for so long that he could not believe how wonderful it was. He felt himself begin to dance, he was so overwhelmed by the colour. He gazed at the fruit in wonder. It was so insignificant - yet now it was so important to him. He knew he desperately needed the vitamins it contained but he could not eat it. The guards were at first puzzled, then angry. Why didn't he eat the fruit? The colour of the fruit had changed everything. The grey prison cell felt less oppressive. Colour and beauty had helped him to cope. Write 'Thank you, God, for orange,' on the strip of paper and place it on the wall.

> Thank you, God, for orange

Prayer/ Reflection

Stand an orange on a table. Place the orange candle in the sand. Light all the candles. Ask the pupils to look at the orange by candle light. After a few seconds ask them to close their eyes.

For all prisoners like Brian Keenan we pray, prisoners deprived of love, light, freedom, and colour. We pray that the innocent may be set free to see again your colourful world.

Note. For guidance on prayers and reflections see pages 9-11.

Remember to extinguish the candles. Make sure all items brought in are safe.

Yellow

Biblical Material: Proverbs 20. 12

These assemblies are a development of the assembly on page 79. They celebrate the colours which Christians believe God put into the world.

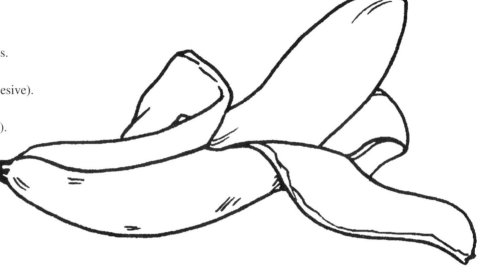

You will need:

- A variety of yellow articles.
- A strip of yellow paper.
- Sticky-Tack (reusable adhesive).
- A large felt-tipped pen.
- A yellow candle (optional).
- Matches (optional).
- A tray of damp sand (optional).
- A line drawing of Judas (provided).

Introduction

Ask the pupils to bring in some yellow items and describe them. They may be bright lemon, gold, pale straw coloured or deep buttery yellow. Make up a 'yellow is ...' poem on the spot. 'Yellow is sunshine.' 'Yellow is sand and holidays' etc.

Core Material

In the Middle Ages, Christian artists used colours to suggest ideas. Artists used two shades of yellow to suggest very different ideas. Gold was the colour of innocence and goodness, and was used for Jesus and the Saints. We also have a saying, 'As good as gold.'

A dingy, dull yellow was used to represent deceit and betrayal. Judas was one of Jesus' disciples. He is often painted in a dull yellow. Judas looked after the money for the other disciples. The Bible says he stole some of the money for himself. Judas started as a friend of Jesus. Eventually, after three years of being his disciple, he betrayed Jesus to his enemies. The painter Giotto painted a picture of Judas betraying Jesus. Jesus and Judas stand in the centre of the painting. Judas is wearing a large dull yellow cloak which he almost wraps round Jesus. Jesus is 'surrounded' by deceit. In the picture Judas is about to kiss Jesus, the normal greeting for a friend, but the kiss is the signal for the soldiers to arrest him. (Mark 14.43-50) The line drawing of Judas and Jesus is included. This can be put on an acetate or be enlarged on the photocopier.

The yellows of creation can remind people that there are choices to be made in life between good and evil, right and wrong. Judas made the wrong choice. Write 'Thank you, God, for yellow,' on the strip of paper and place it on the wall.

> Thank you, God, for yellow

Prayer/Reflection

Place the yellow candle in the sand. Light all the candles. Ask pupils to think of people who they know who are as 'good as gold'.

Father as we look on your world help us to be attracted to the goodness that shines more brightly than gold.

Note. For guidance on prayers and reflections see pages 9-11.

Remember to extinguish the candles. Make sure all items brought in are safe.

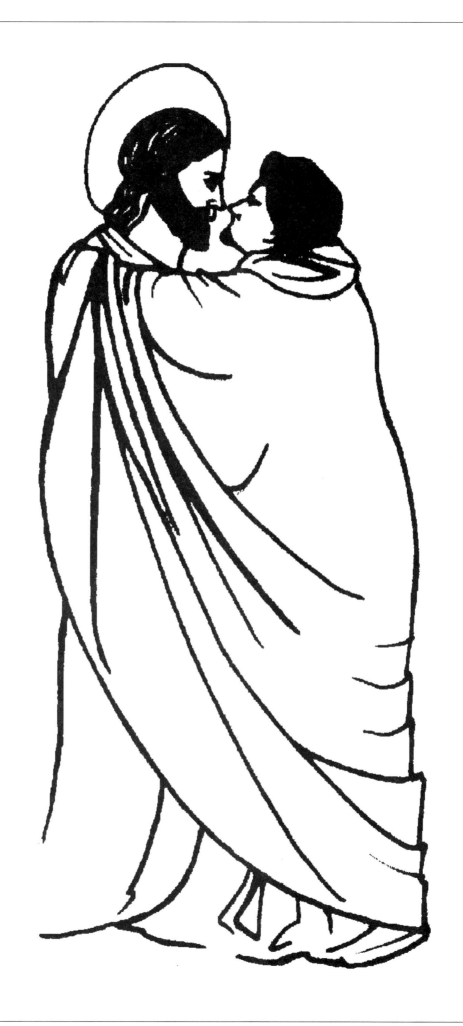

Green

Biblical Material: Proverbs 20. 12

These assemblies are a development of the assembly on page 79. They celebrate the colours which Christians believe God put into the world.

You will need:

- A variety of green articles.
- A strip of green paper.
- A large felt-tipped pen.
- Sticky-Tack (reusable adhesive).
- A green candle (optional).
- A tray of damp sand (optional).
- Matches (optional).
- Sheets of coloured paper.

Introduction

Ask the pupils to bring in some green items and describe them. Are they bright lime greens, apple green or deep bottle green? Use the coloured paper to 'test' for restful colours. What colour would they paint a room to make it restful?

Core Material

Green is the basic clothing of the world, the main colour of plants. Looking out over a green landscape is restful. Think how hard on the eyes it would be if the fields were all different shades of orange! You would need sunglasses. Scientists have discovered that green is a restful colour. Christians believe God knew that a long time ago! Write 'Thank you, God, for green,' on the strip of paper and place it on the wall.

> Thank you, God, for green

Prayer/Reflection

Place the green candle in the sand. Light all the candles. Pupils can listen prayerfully to the poem 'Green Blackboards' by Michel Quoist.

The school is up-to-date.

Proudly, the principal tells of all the improvements.

The finest discovery, Lord, is the green blackboard.

The scientists have studied long, they have made experiments;

We know now that green is the ideal colour, that it doesn't tire the eyes, that it is quieting and relaxing.

It has occurred to me, Lord, that you didn't wait so long to paint the trees and the meadows green.

Your research laboratories were efficient, and in order not to tire us, you perfected a number of shades of green for your modern meadows.

And so the 'finds' of men consist in discovering what you have known from time immemorial.

Thank you, Lord, for being the good Father who gives his children the joy of discovering by themselves the treasures of his intelligence and love,

But keep us from believing that - by ourselves - we have invented anything at all.

Note. For guidance on prayers and reflections see pages 9-11.

Remember to extinguish the candles and make sure all items brought in are safe.

Blue

Biblical Material: Proverbs 20. 12

These assemblies are a development of the assembly on page 79. They celebrate the colours which Christians believe God put into the world.

You will need:

- A variety of blue articles.
- A strip of blue paper.
- A large felt tipped pen.
- Sticky-Tack (reusable adhesive).
- A blue candle (optional).
- A tray of damp sand (optional).
- Matches (optional).

Introduction

Ask the pupils to bring in some blue items and describe them. Are they navy or sky blue? Are they cornflower blue or royal blue? Try inventing names for shades of blue as they do for paint. Names such as 'moonlight blue'. Pupils can make up names and describe the shade of blue.

Core Material

Colours are not only for decoration: they can affect our moods. If the sky is always a dark grey, it can make you feel gloomy. A bright blue sky and sunny day can make you feel hopeful. Careful use of colour can make rooms feel cheerful and warm, cool or inviting. In Medieval times, colours were used in Christian paintings as a type of code. Each colour carried a message or had a special meaning. Blue was the colour of heavenly love. That is why Mary is often painted wearing a blue dress in pictures of the Christmas story. Mary was painted wearing blue because she was the Mother of Jesus.

Christians believe Jesus came to show God's love. Write 'Thank you, God, for blue,' on the strip of paper and place it on the wall.

> Thank you, God, for blue

Prayer/Reflection

Add the blue candle to the sand. Light all the candles. The pupils can think of different blues while the prayer is read.

Thank you, God, for blue, the colour of love.
Thank you that the sky,
The flowers, and all of
your blue creation
Can remind us of
your love.

Note.
For guidance on prayers and reflections see pages 9-11.
Remember to extinguish the candles. Make sure all items brought in are safe.

Indigo (purple)

Biblical Material: Proverbs 20.12

These assemblies are a development of the assembly on page 79. They celebrate the colours which Christians believe God put into the world.

You will need:

- A variety of indigo/purple articles.
- A strip of indigo/purple paper.
- A large felt-tipped pen.
- Sticky-Tack (reusable adhesive).
- A indigo/purple candle (optional).
- A tray of damp sand (optional).
- Matches (optional).
- An onion.

Introduction

Ask the pupils to bring in some indigo/purple items and describe them. Indigo is a deep purplish blue or bluish purple. It is a deeper colour than violet. Pupils may wish to describe their coloured items. Some plums are indigo, as are aubergines and certain types of pansies. Talk about the different plants and berries which produce dye such as onion skins. Pupils can suggest other plants which might give dye and the colour they would produce.

Core Material

Indigo dye is made from a plant. It could be called the 'poor man's purple' because it is a fairly cheap dye to produce. Long ago, few people wore purple because it cost so much to produce. In the time of Jesus, true purple was only worn by the very rich and important. True purple, or 'Tyrian purple' as it was called, was obtained from a snail called the murex. Each snail gave only a few drops of dye which made true purple dye extremely expensive. In Roman times, the Emperor wore true purple. Ordinary people used other colours which were cheaper.

Christian painters used purple to indicate God the Father. Just as the ruler of the Roman world, the Emperor, could wear true purple, so Christians painted God wearing purple to express their belief that he was the real ruler of the world. In nature, things coloured indigo or purple are rare, but the dark colour adds variety and contrast. Without it, yellow and white would not look as bright. Write 'Thank you, God, for indigo,' on the strip of paper and place it on the wall.

> Thank you, God, for indigo

Prayer/Reflection

Add the indigo/purple candle to the sand. Light all the candles. Pupils can think of different shades of purple while the prayer is read.

For Royal purple that reminds us you are King, we thank you, God.

For the purple of plums, The velvet of pansies, The egg-like aubergine.

For your rarer colours, God, we thank you -

Note. For guidance on prayers and reflections see pages 9-11.

Remember to extinguish the candles. Make sure all items brought in are safe.

Violet

Biblical Material: Proverbs 20. 12

These assemblies are a development of the assembly on page 79. They celebrate the colours which Christians believe God put into the world.

You will need:

- A variety of violet articles.
- A strip of violet paper.
- A large felt tipped pen.
- Sticky-Tack (reusable adhesive).
- A violet candle (optional).
- A tray of damp sand (optional).
- Matches (optional).

Introduction

Ask the pupils to bring in some violet items and describe them. Violet is a lighter shade of purple. Like true purple, it is not a common colour. Some flowers come in many shades of violet. Spend time recapping over the complete rainbow. Play rainbow 'I spy', working through all the colours.

Core Material

Some churches use violet to represent truth and suffering. Violet is used before Christmas (during Advent) and before Easter (during Lent) in certain churches. At Advent, Christians remember Jesus came as a baby in a poor family and lived as a human being. Christians believe he knew love, sorrow, joy and suffering just as we do. That is why violet coloured candles are often used in an Advent ring. At Lent, Christians remember Jesus' death. This is why violet is used in church fabric before Easter. If you look at the stand in the pulpit on which the minister/priest rests the Bible, it may have a violet cloth on it in Lent. The Bible may also have a violet book mark.

By looking at the violet objects in the world Christians may be reminded of Jesus' suffering and all those who suffer for the truth. Write 'Thank you, God, for violet,' on the strip of paper and place it on the wall.

> Thank you, God, for violet

Prayer/Reflection

Place the violet candle in the sand.
Light all the candles.
There should now be a rainbow of paper and candles.
Pupils can recall all the colours while the prayer is read.

For all things violet,
We thank you, God.

For nature's reminder
Of truth and suffering,
We thank you, God.

Help us never to take peace and security for granted.

Note.
For guidance on prayers and reflections see pages 9-11.
Remember to extinguish the candles and make sure all items brought in are safe.

Music Index: suggested hymns and songs

Note: when a song or hymn is particularly suitable for a specific assembly, the assembly's number appears in brackets after the song or hymn.

WORDS, WORDS, WORDS

You can build a wall. *Come and Praise 2*

God bless the grass (3). *Someone's Singing, Lord*

I am the way, the truth and the life (3). *Sing to God*

Make me a channel of your peace (5). *Alleluya*

Guantanamera (8). *Alleluya*

JUST THINKING ABOUT IT

Think, think on these things. *Someone's Singing, Lord*

New every morning. *Junior Praise*

Fill thou my life. *Come and Praise 1*

May the mind (10). *Junior Praise*

He who would valiant be (11). *Junior Praise*

Teach me, my God and King (12). *Junior Praise*

I want to walk with Jesus Christ (13). *Junior Praise*

Search me, O God (13). *Junior Praise*

THINGS TO AVOID

You can build a wall. *Come and Praise 2*

Jesus, humble was your birth. *Sing to God*

Father, lead me day by day. *Junior Praise*

Simple gifts (14). *Come and Praise 2*

Give me oil (16). *Junior Praise*

If you see someone (16). *Junior Praise*

The angry song (21). *Tinderbox*

WEALTH AND POVERTY

Now we sing a harvest song. *Praise God Together*

Guantanamera. *Alleluya*

When I needed a neighbour. *Come and Praise 2*

Magic Penny. *Alleluya*

God who put the stars in space. *Someone's Singing, Lord*

Simple gifts (22). *Come and Praise 2*

O Lord! Shout for joy (22). *Someone's Singing, Lord*

I want to live for Jesus every day (24). *Junior Praise, Come and Praise 2*

Our Father God who gives to me (26). *Sing to God*

Cross over the road (26). *Praise God Together*

THE GOOD THINGS IN LIFE

When your Father made the world. *Come and Praise 2*

Peace, perfect peace (27). *Come and Praise 1*

Love will never come to an end (28). *Come and Praise 2*

I may speak (28). *Come and Praise 2*
The wise may bring their learning (29). *Sing to God*
I'll sing your praise (29). *Many Ways to Praise*
From the tiny ant (30). *Come and Praise 1*
All the animals (30). *Come and Praise 2*
A better world (32). *Alleluya*
Spirit of God (35). *Come and Praise 1*
Cross over (35). *Come and Praise 1*
Make me a channel of your peace (36). *Alleluya*
This little light of mine (37). *Alleluya*
I am a lighthouse (37). *Junior Praise*

EDUCATION

The builders. *Many Ways to Praise*
The journey of life (39). *Praise God Together*
Christ be my leader (39). *Praise God Together*
The building song (40). *Alleluya*

LIVING WITH TOMORROW

Turn, turn, turn. *Alleluya*
Lord, I love to stamp and shout. *Someone's Singing, Lord*
I watch the sunrise (41). *Alleluya*
Raindrops keep falling on my head (41). *Alleluya*
Each day different (42). *Harlequin*
Give us hope, Lord (43). *Come and Praise 1*
Peace, perfect peace (43). *Come and Praise 1*
Spirit of peace (43). *Come and Praise 2*

THE UPS AND DOWNS OF LIFE

O Jesus, I have promised. *Sing to God*
Dear Lord and Father of mankind. *Junior Praise*
Think, think. *Someone's Singing, Lord.*
Forbidden fruit (44). *Sing-Song Roundabout: Praise Away*
Learning to be good is hard (45). *Sing-Song-Roundabout: Praise Away*
It's always them (47). *Sing-Song-Roundabout: Praise Away*
Look into your heart (47). *Sing-Song-Roundabout*
Speck, speck, speck (47 and 49). *Praise God Together*
Sing life, sing love (48). *Praise God Together*
Right side up (48). *Praise God Together*
Seek ye first the kingdom of God (50). *Junior Praise*
God loves a cheerful giver (50). *Alleluya*
Blowing in the wind (51). *Alleluya*
Father, hear the prayer we offer (51). *Sing to God*
Should I turn about? (52). *Sing-Song-Roundabout: Praise Away*
It's me, it's me, it's me, O Lord (52). *Junior Praise*
Cleanse me from my sin, Lord (53). *Junior Praise*
I'm special (53). *Junior Praise*

SEVEN THINGS THAT GOD DOES NOT TOLERATE

Right side up. *Praise God Together*

In our work and in our play. *Sing to God*

Learning to be good is hard. *Sing-Song-Roundabout: Praise Away*

This train is bound for glory. *Alleluya*

In our work and in our play (54). *Junior Praise*

Where have all the flowers gone? (57). *Alleluya*

Lord of the loving heart (58 and 59). *Sing to God*

Jesus' hands were kind hands (58). *Junior Praise*

GOD'S WORLD

Stand up, clap hands (62). *Come and Sing Some More*

When I see the salmon (62). *Praise God Together*

Music of the world (62). *Alleluya*

Give to us eyes (63). *Praise God Together*

I sing a song of the saints (64). *Junior Praise*

Who put the colours in the rainbow? (65 or 62). *Praise God Together*

Rainbow harvest (65 or 62). *Sing-Song-Roundabout: Songs for a Year*

Song of Caedmon (67). *Come and Praise 1*

Think of a world (67). *Junior Praise*

You can't stop God from loving you (68). *Junior Praise*

He's got the whole wide world (69). *Junior Praise*

To God be the glory (69). *Junior Praise*

There is a green hill (70). *Junior Praise*

BOOKS REFERRED TO IN THE MUSIC INDEX

Alleluya   chosen by D. Gadsby and J. Hoggarth, A.and C. Black, '82

Praise God Together   comp. M.V. Old, S.U. '84

Come and Sing Some More   comp. A. Broad, S.U. '88

Many Ways to Praise   comp. S. Sayers, Palm Tree Press, '86

Sing to God   comp. M. V. Old, and E. M. Stephenson S. U. '79

Sing-Song-Roundabout: Praise Away   B. Piper and F. Cooke, Longman '89

Sing-Song-Roundabout: Songs for a Year   Rosemary Barralet Bunbury, Longman '88

Come and Praise 1 comp.   G. Marshall-Taylor, B.B.C. Publications '78

Come and Praise 2 comp.   G. Marshall-Taylor, B.B.C. Publications '88

Junior Praise comp.   P. Horrobin and G. Leavers, Marshall Pickering '86

Tinderbox   chosen by S. Barratt and S. Hodge, A. and C. Black '82

Someone's Singing Lord   chosen by S. Barratt and S. Hodge, A. and C. Black '73

Harlequin   chosen by D. Gadsby and B. Harrap, A. and C. Black '81